BILLIARDS
NOTE 1.0
아라의 당구홀릭©
닿끝

아라의 당구홀릭
당구노트

© 아라 & 폴, 2017

1판 1쇄 발행 __ 2017년 01월 20일
1판 2쇄 발행 __ 2020년 10월 30일

지은이 __ 아라 & 폴
펴낸이 __ 홍정표

펴낸곳 __ 글로벌콘텐츠
   등록 __ 제 25100-2008-000024호

공급처 __ (주)글로벌콘텐츠출판그룹
   대표 __ 홍정표 **이사** __ 김미미 **편집** __ 권군오 김수아 하선연 이상민 홍명지 **기획·마케팅** __ 이종훈
   주소 __ 서울특별시 강동구 풍성로 87-5 **전화** __ 02-488-3280 **팩스** __ 02-488-3281
   홈페이지 __ www.gcbook.co.kr

정가 10,000원

·이 책은 본사와 저자의 허락 없이는 내용의 일부 또는 전체를 무단 전재나 복제, 광전자 매체 수록 등을 금합니다.
·잘못된 책은 구입처에서 바꾸어 드립니다.

파이브 & 하프 시스템(5 & Half System)

3쿠션 게임에서 가장 많이 사용하는 시스템이며 반드시 익혀야 할 시스템 중 하나이다.

〈큐볼값과 제1쿠션값〉

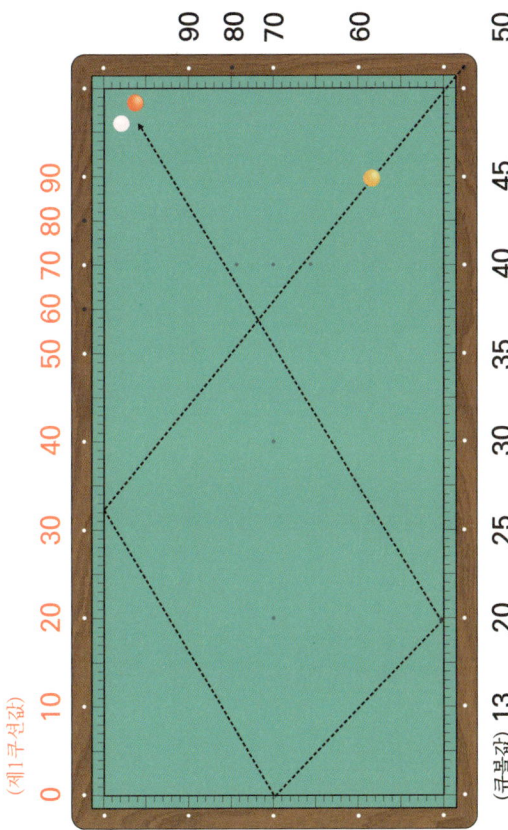

파이브 & 하프 시스템 (5 & Half System)

〈제3쿠션→제4쿠션 도착지점값〉

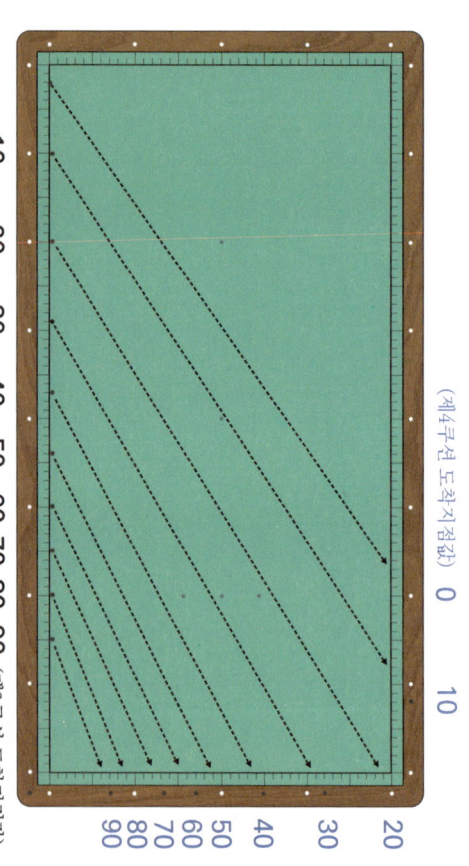

〈공식: 큐볼값-제4쿠션도착지점값= 제1쿠션값〉

50 - 20 = 30

(사용당점)

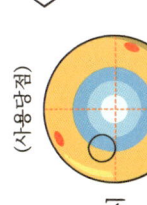

9시

(제1쿠션값) 30

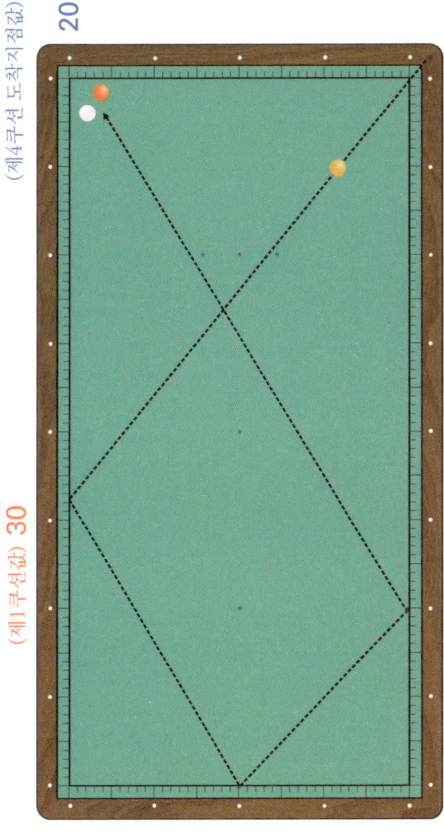

(제4쿠션 도착지점값) 20

(큐볼값) 50

(제3쿠션 도착지점값) 20

완전 쉬운 짧은 각 보정법!!

장축 전체 거리값을 10등분하여 큐볼의 위치에 해당하는 값만큼 빼줄 것!!

30-20=10-5=5

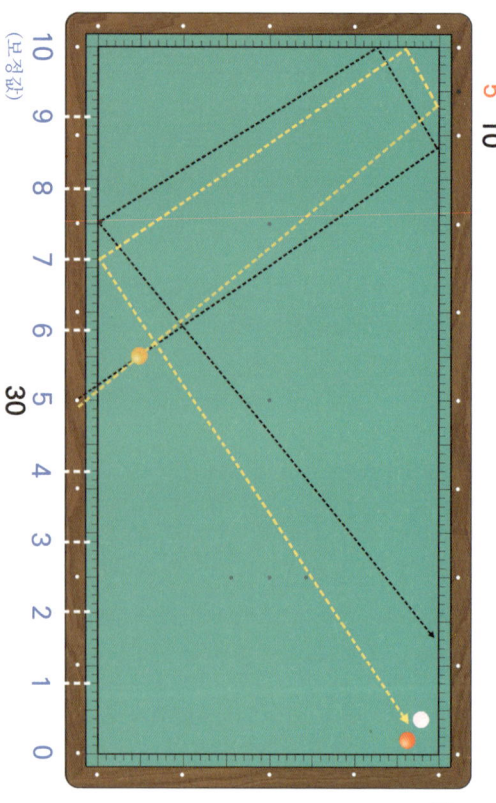

완전 쉬운 긴 각 보정법!!

단축 전체 거리값을 10등분하여 큐볼의 위치에 해당하는 값만큼 더해줄 것!!

$$60 - 30 = 30 + 2.5 = 32.5$$

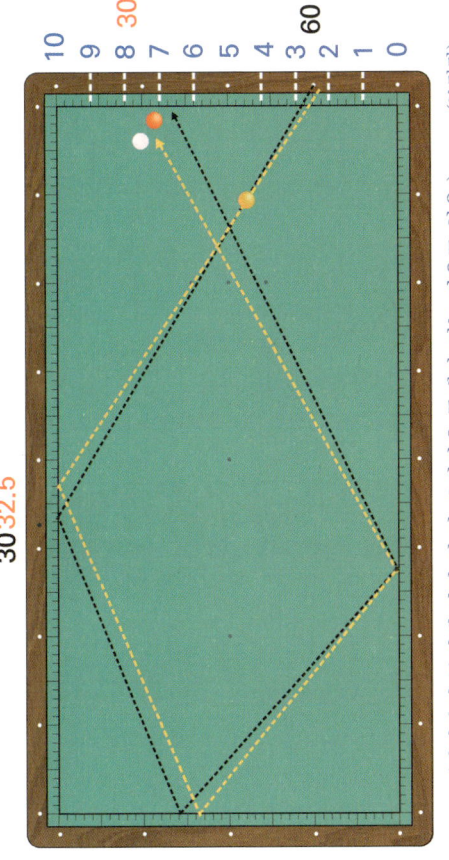

Date: Position:

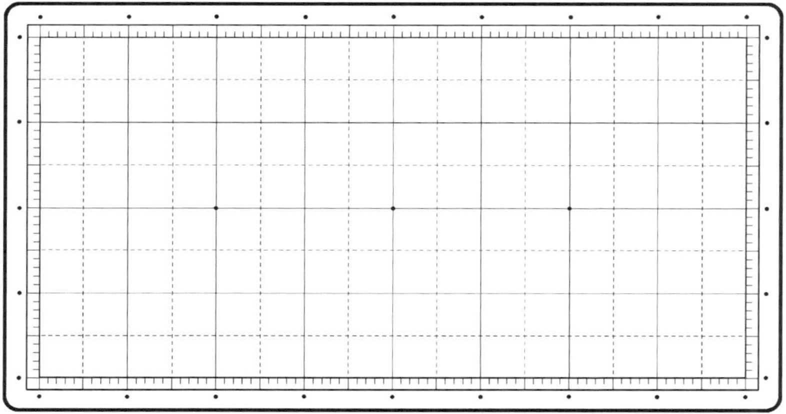

Point:

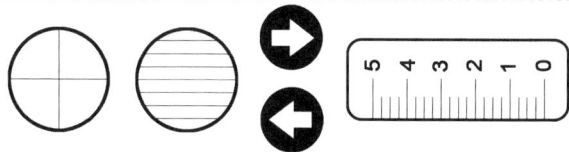

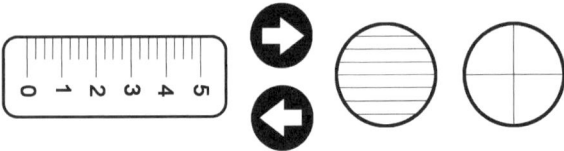

Date: Position:

Point:

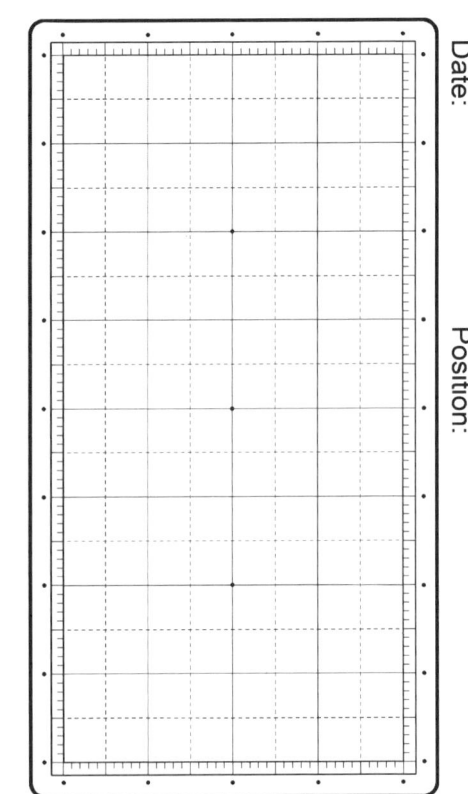

Date: Position:

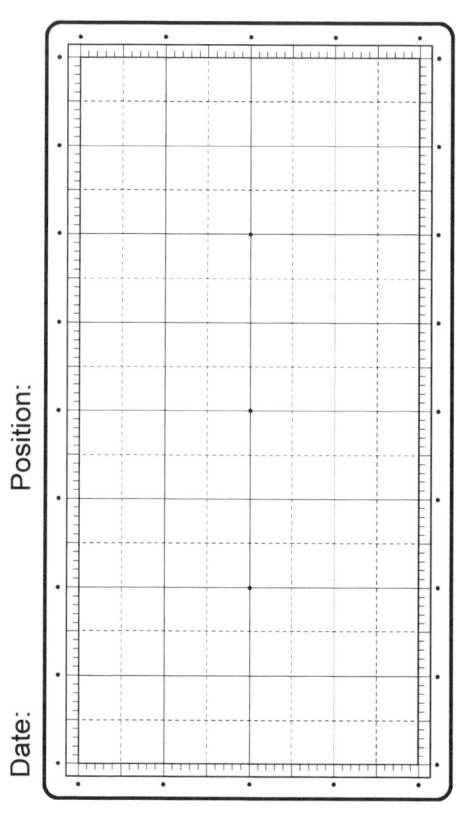

Point:

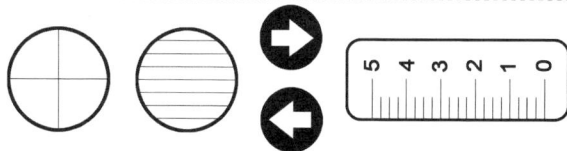

Date: Position:

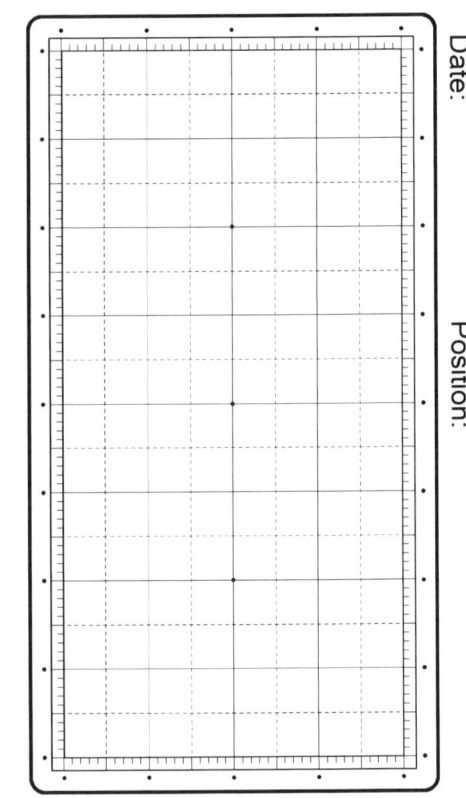

Point:

Date: Position:

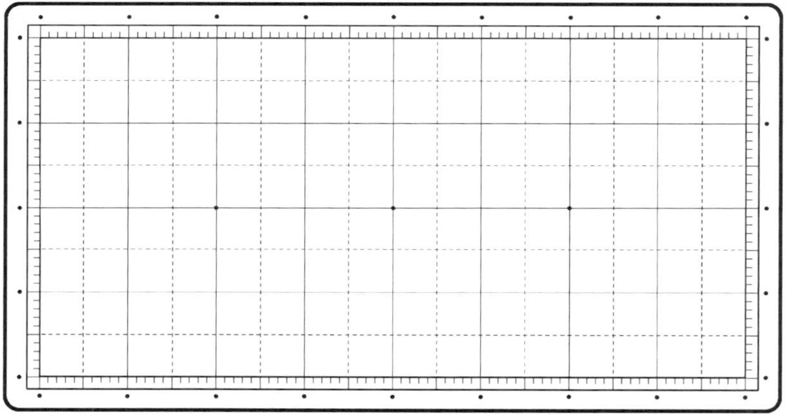

Point:

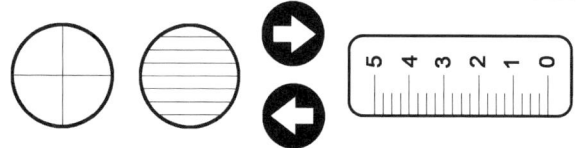

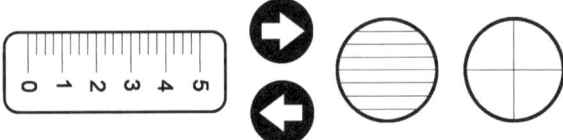

Date: Position:

Point:

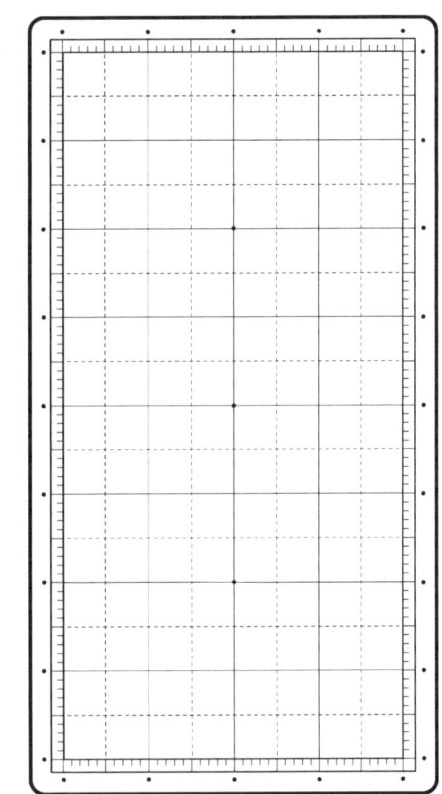

Date: Position:

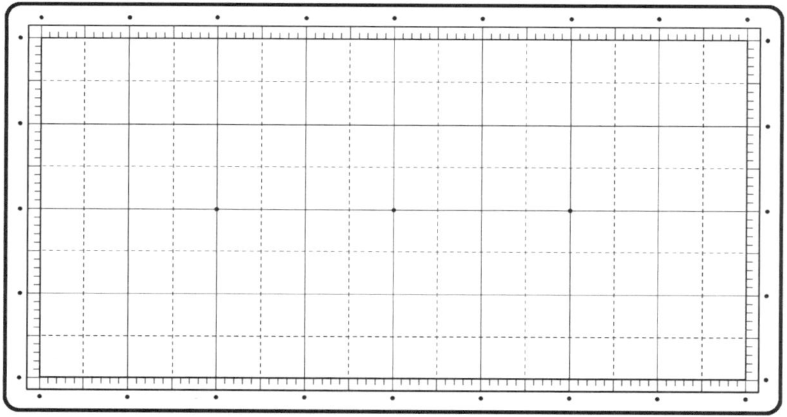

Point:

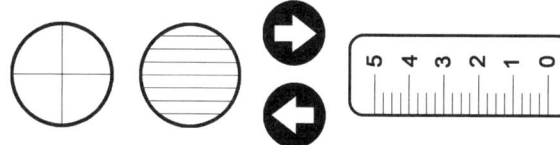

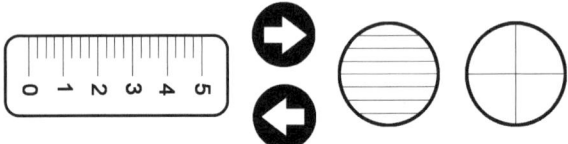

Date:

Position:

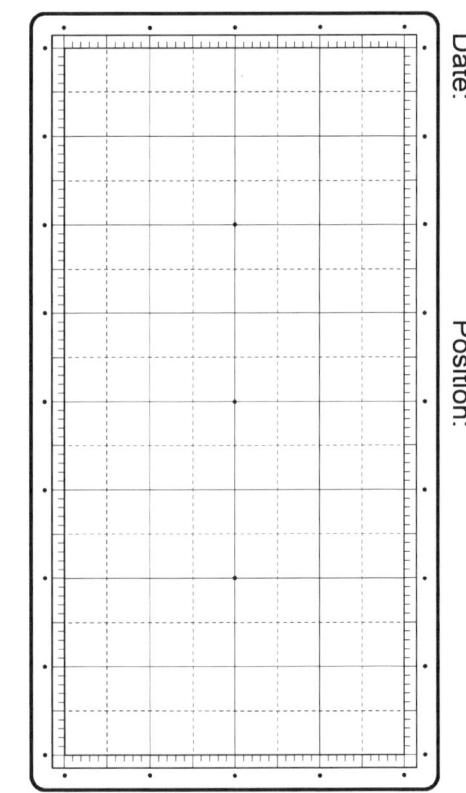

Point:

Date: Position:

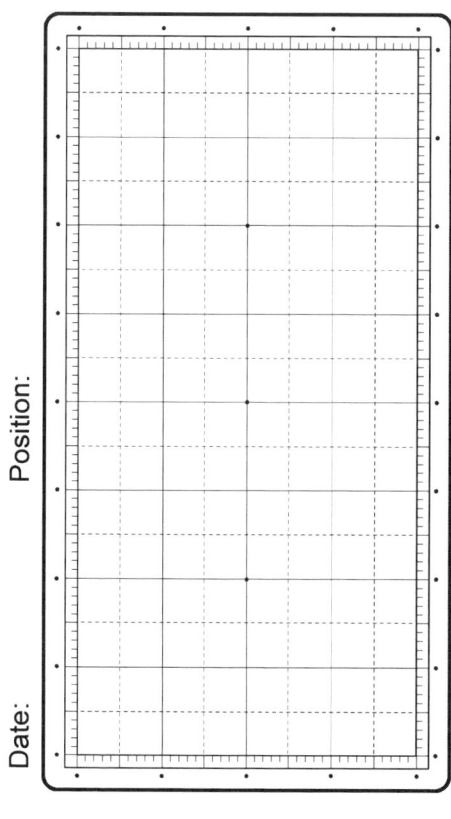

Point:

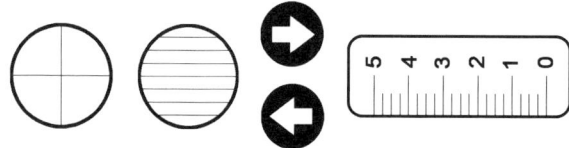

Date: Position:

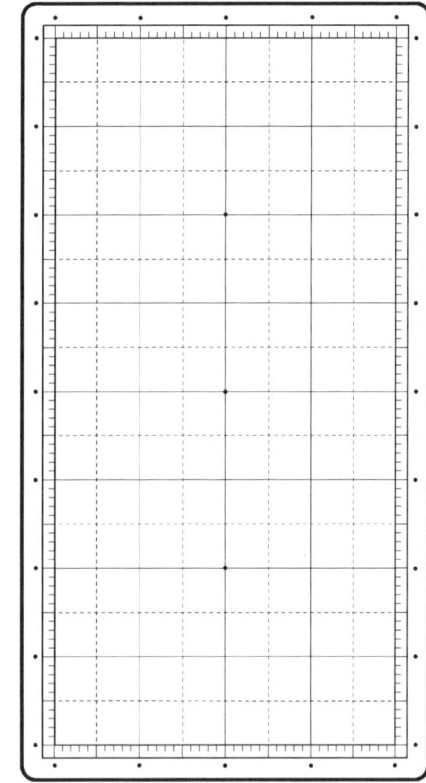

Point:

Date: Position:

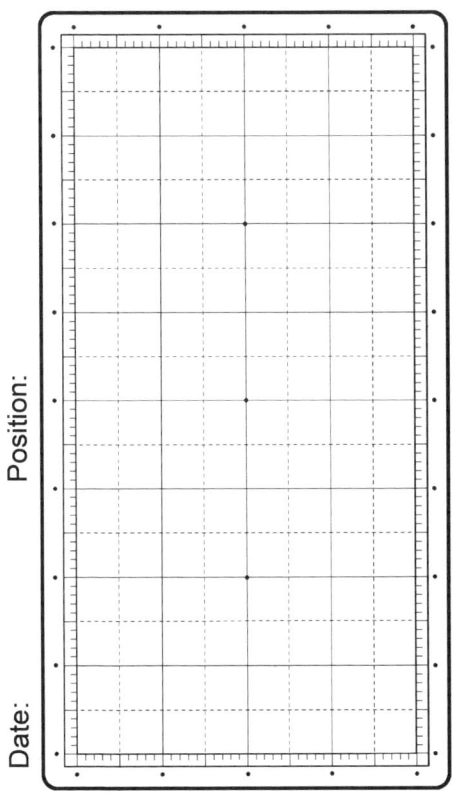

Point:

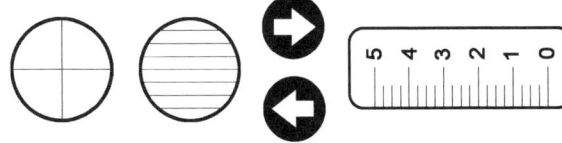

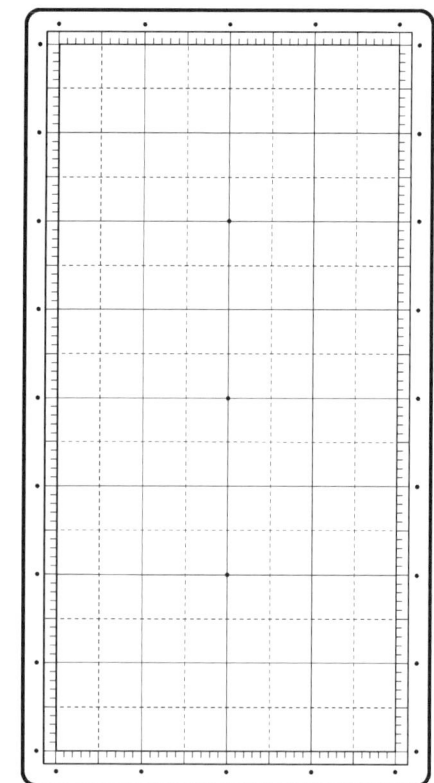

Date:

Position:

Point:

Date: Position:

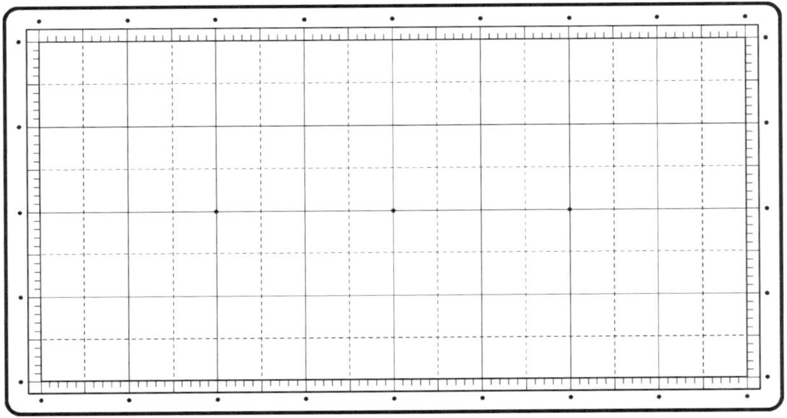

Point:

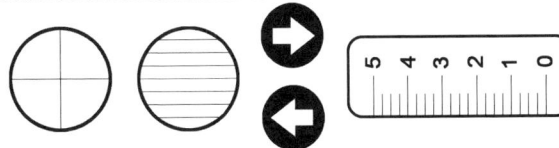

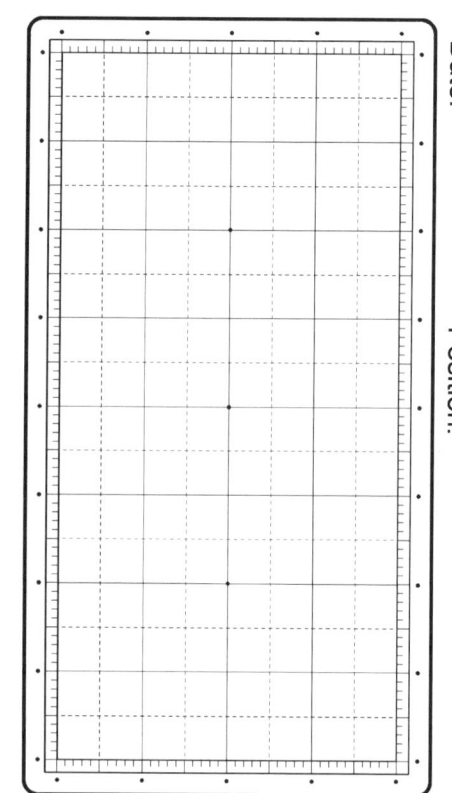

Date:

Position:

Point:

Date: Position:

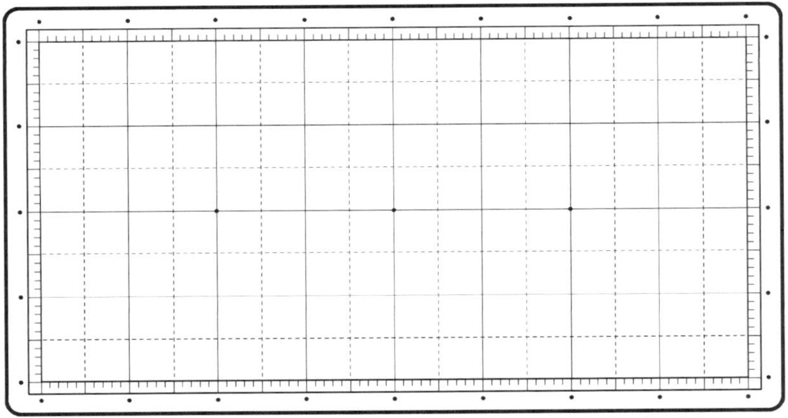

Point:

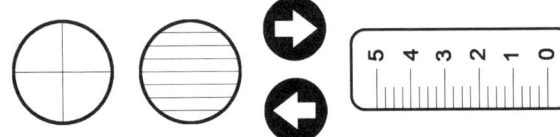

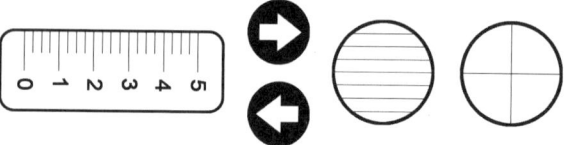

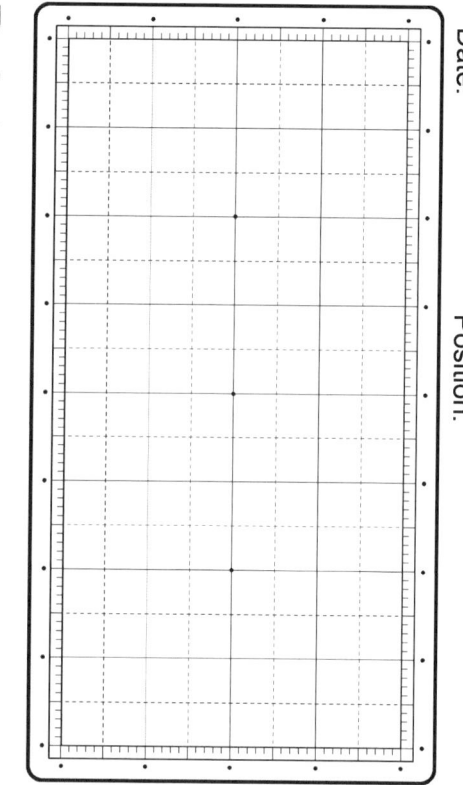

Date:

Position:

Point:

Date: Position:

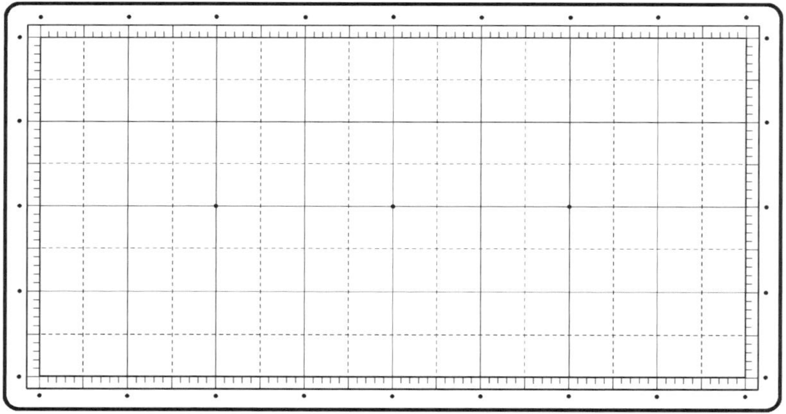

Point:

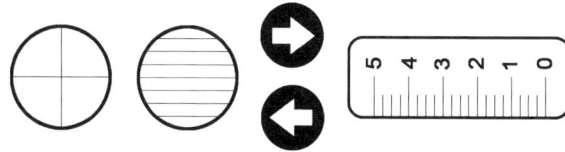

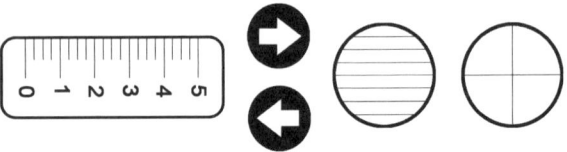

Date: Position:

Point:

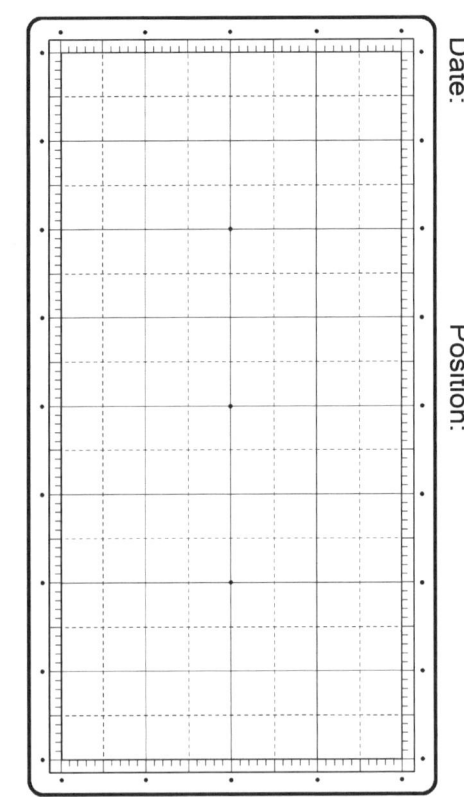

Date: Position:

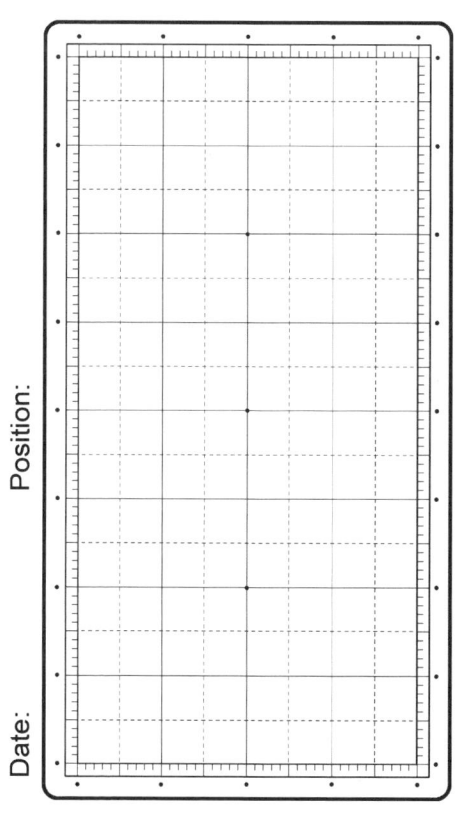

Point:

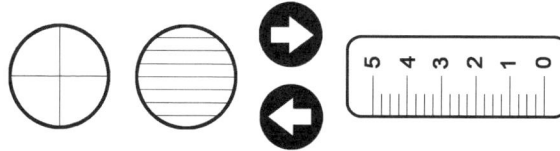

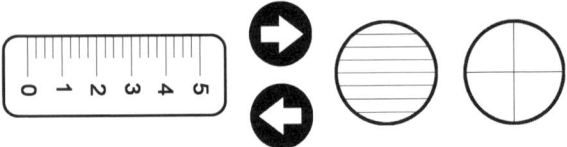

Date:

Position:

Point:

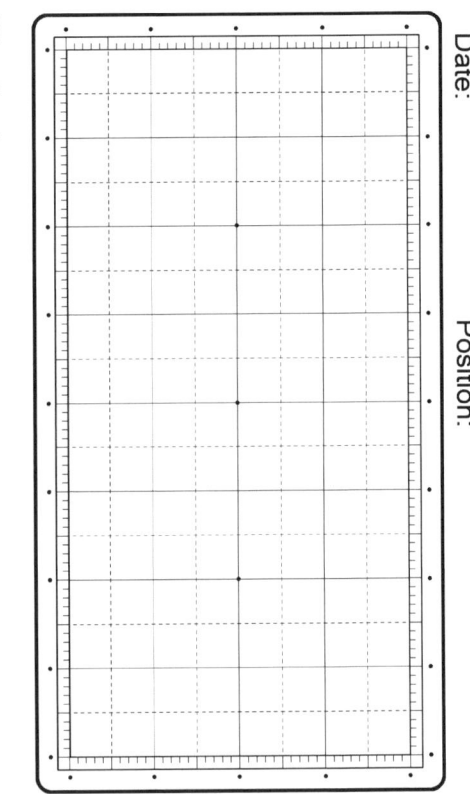

Date: Position:

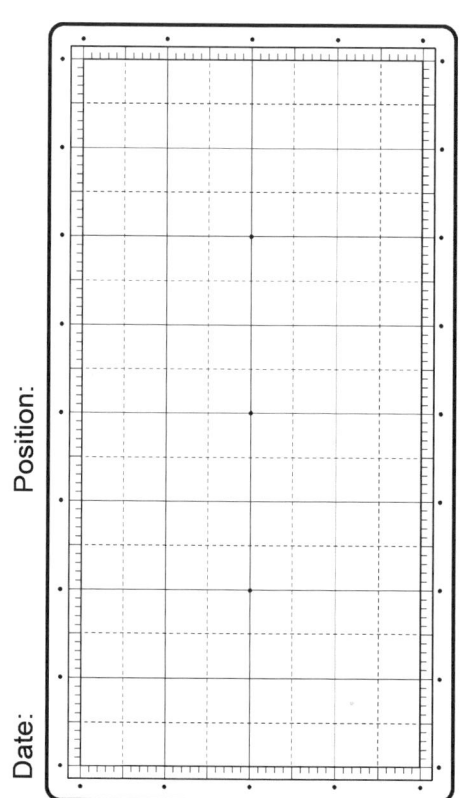

Point:

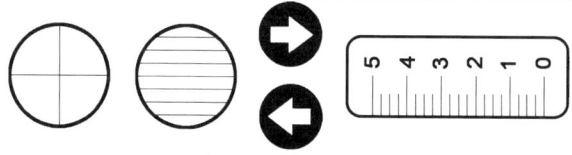

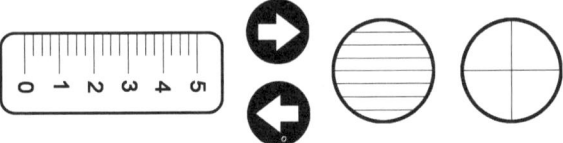

Date: Position:

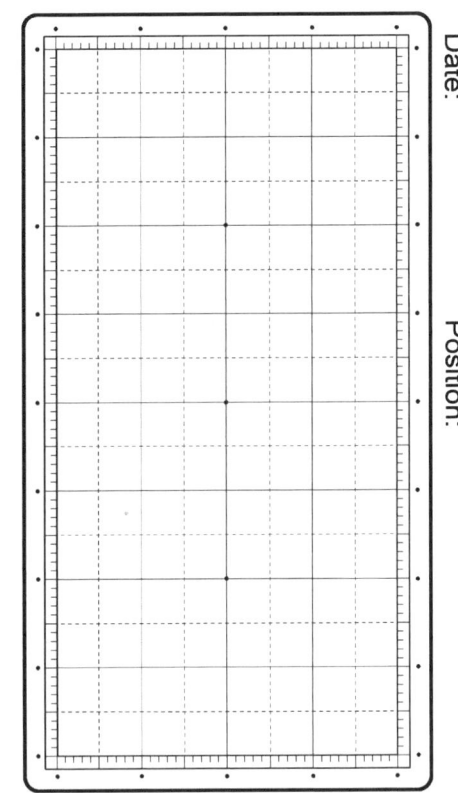

Point:

Date: Position:

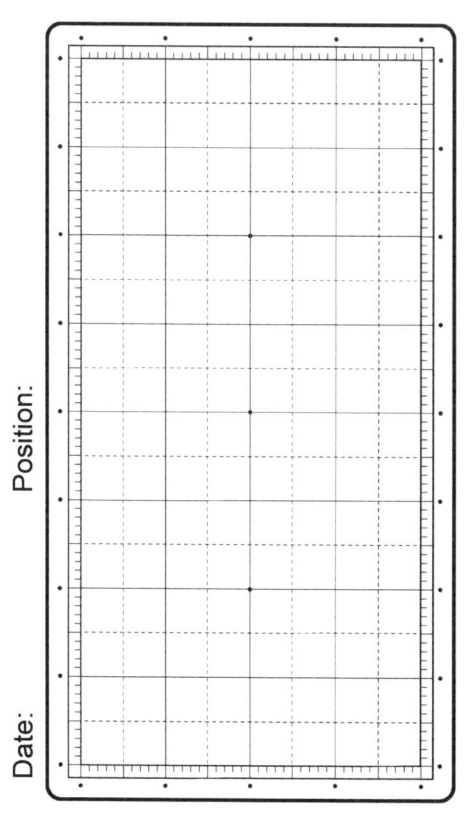

Point:

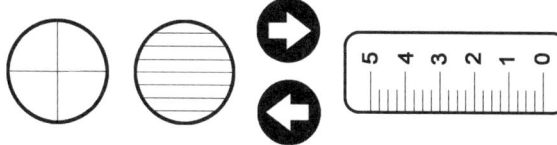

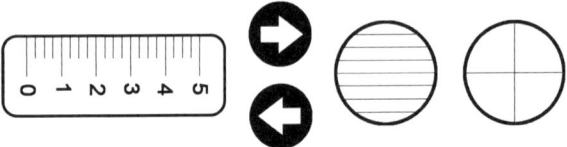

Date: Position:

Point:

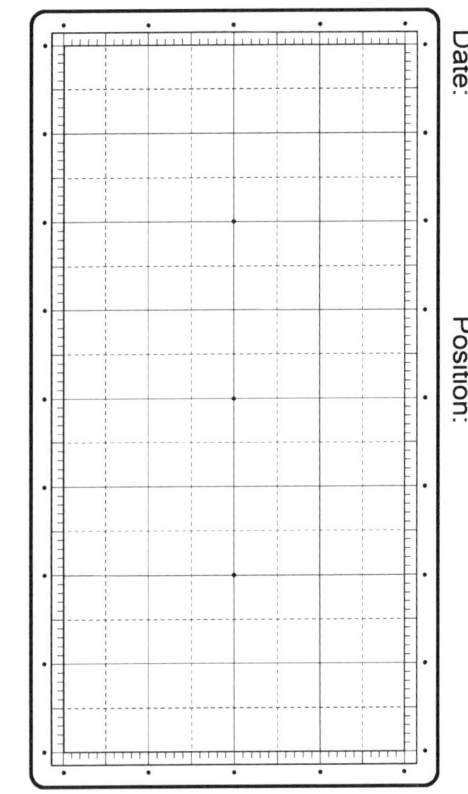

Date: Position:

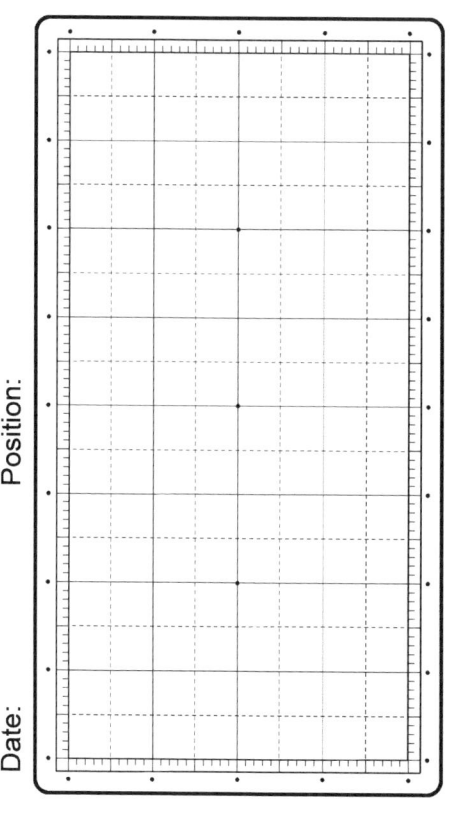

Point:

Date: Position:

Point:

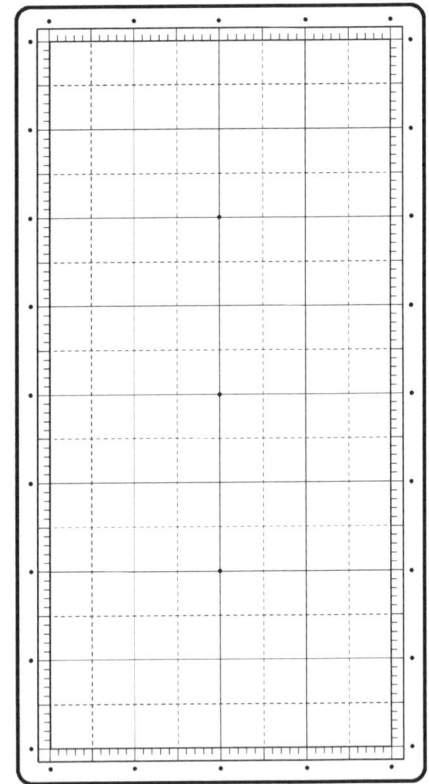

Date: Position:

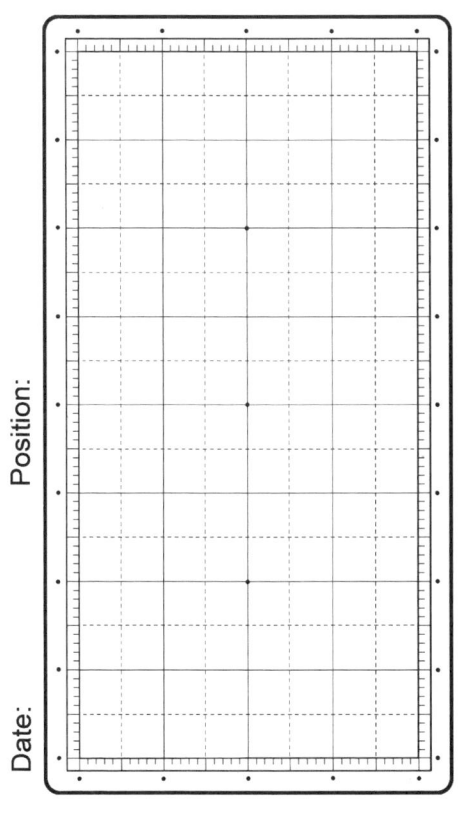

Point:

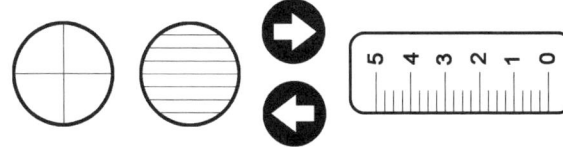

Date: Position:

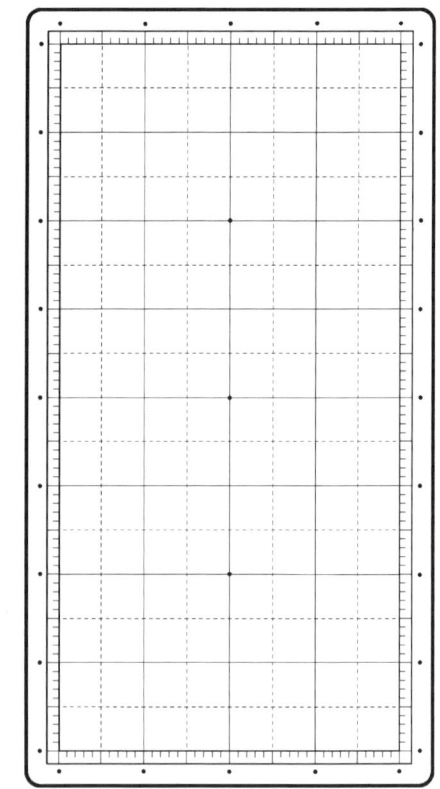

Point:

Date: Position:

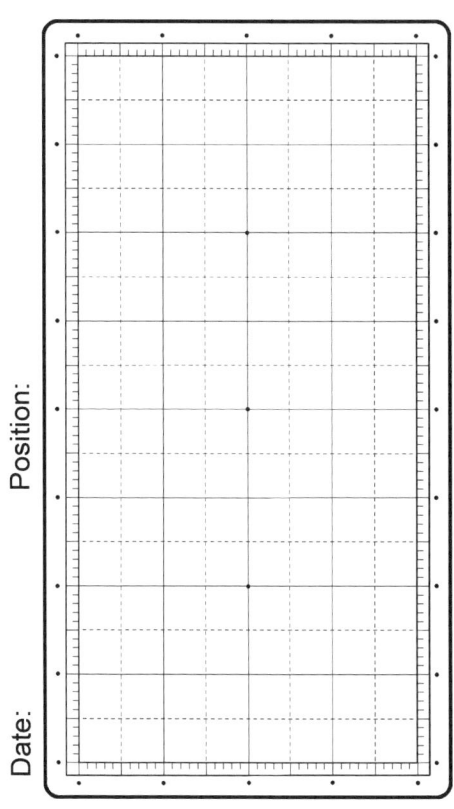

Point:

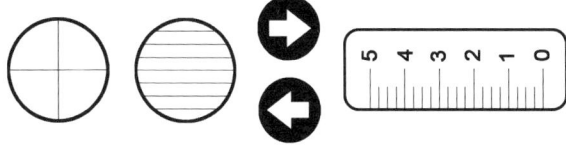

Point:

Date:

Position:

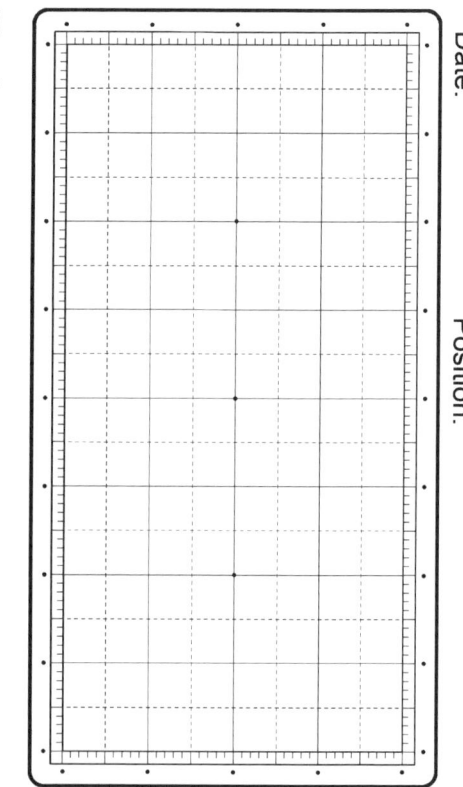

Date: Position:

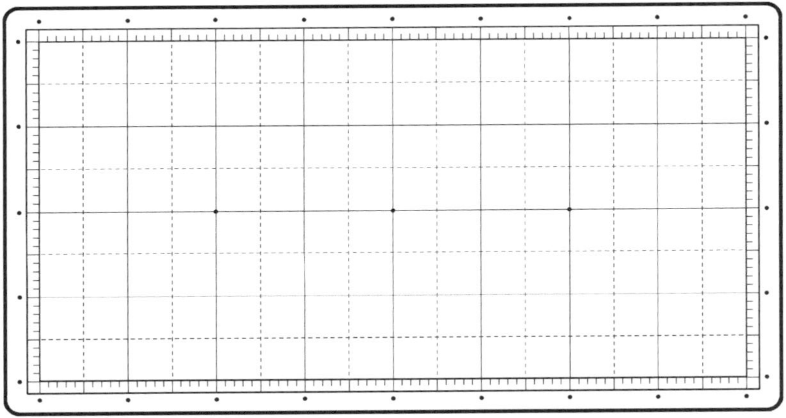

Point:

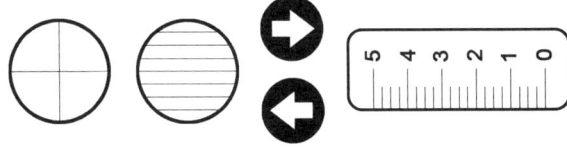

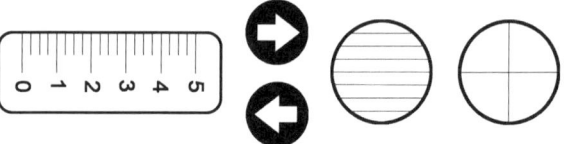

Date:

Position:

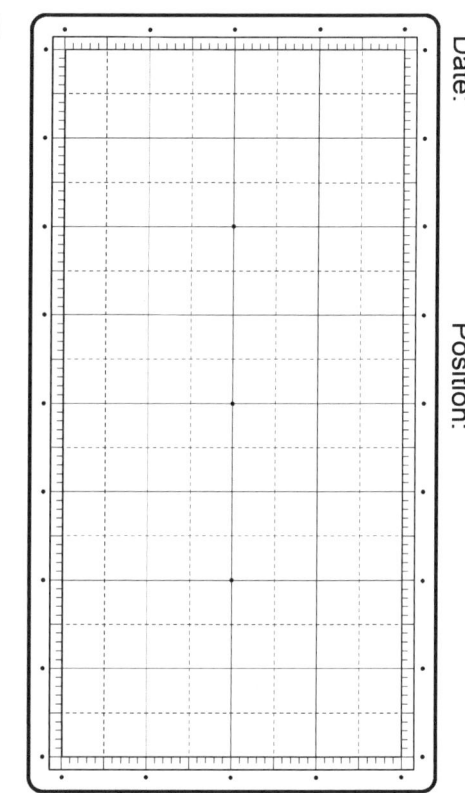

Point:

Date:

Position:

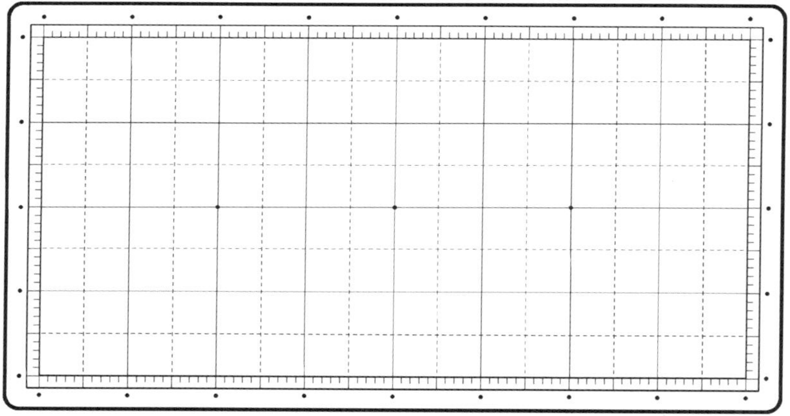

Point:

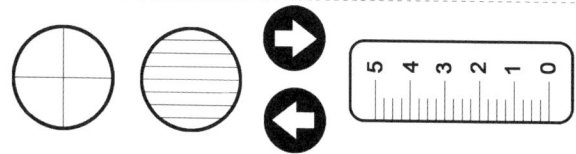

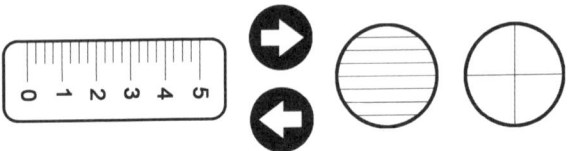

Date:

Position:

Point:

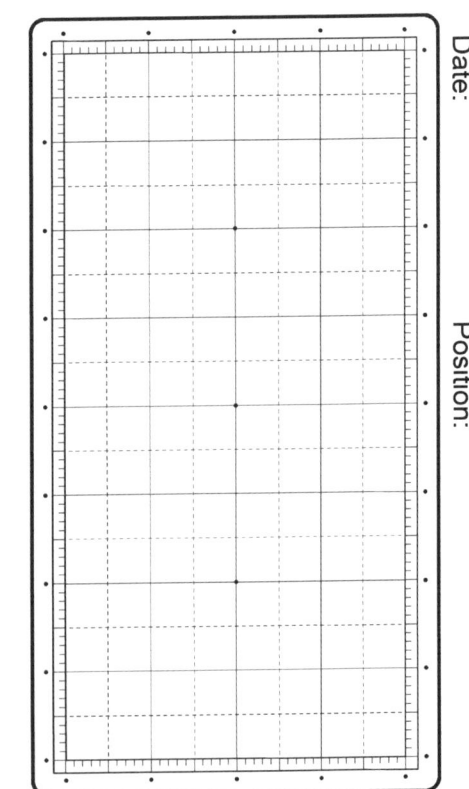

Date: Position:

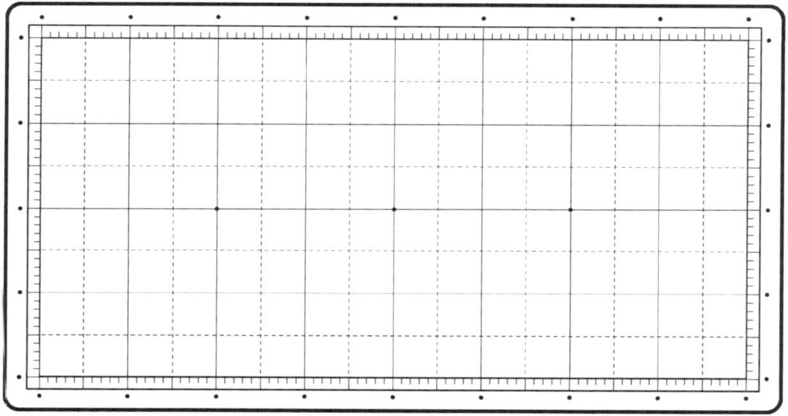

Point:

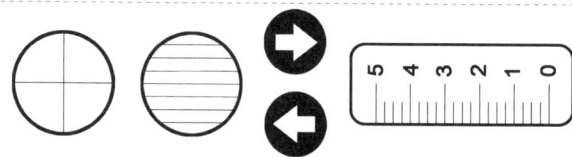

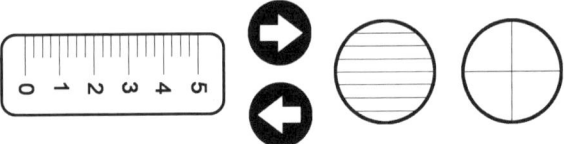

Date: Position:

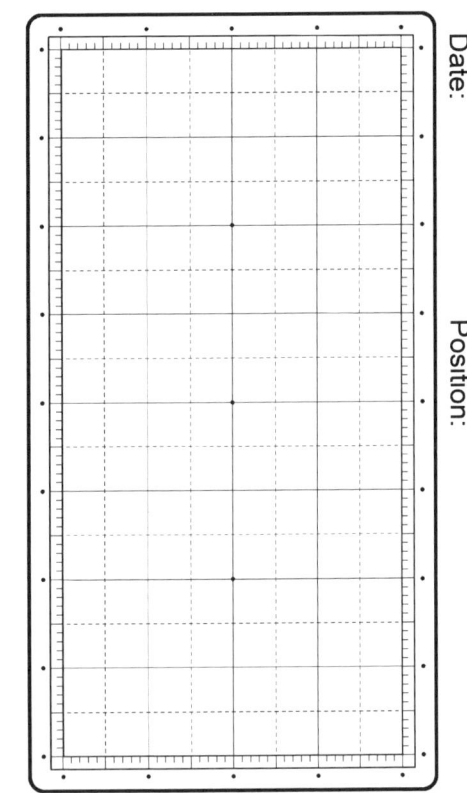

Point:

Date: Position:

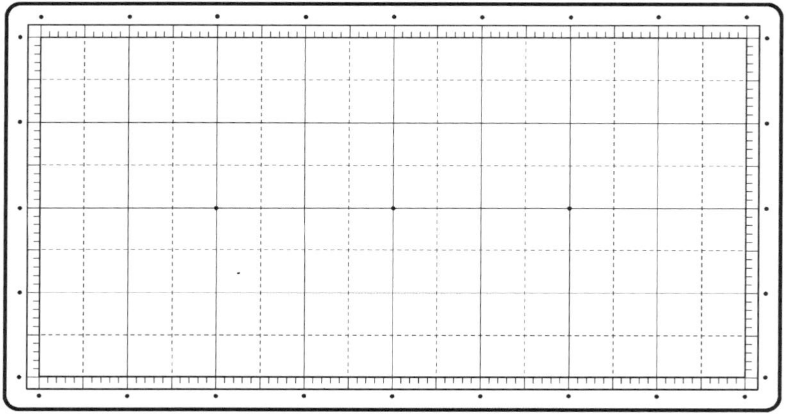

Point:

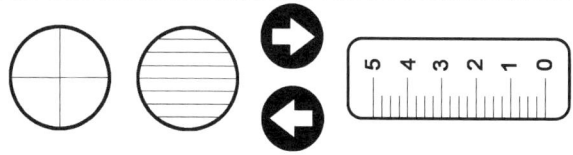

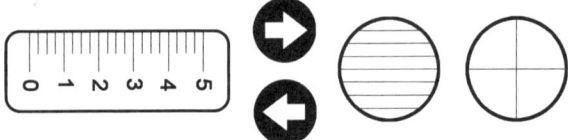

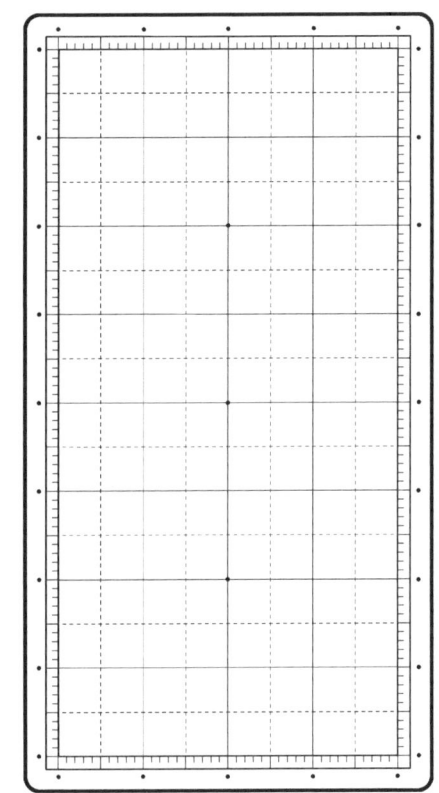

Date:

Position:

Point:

Date: Position:

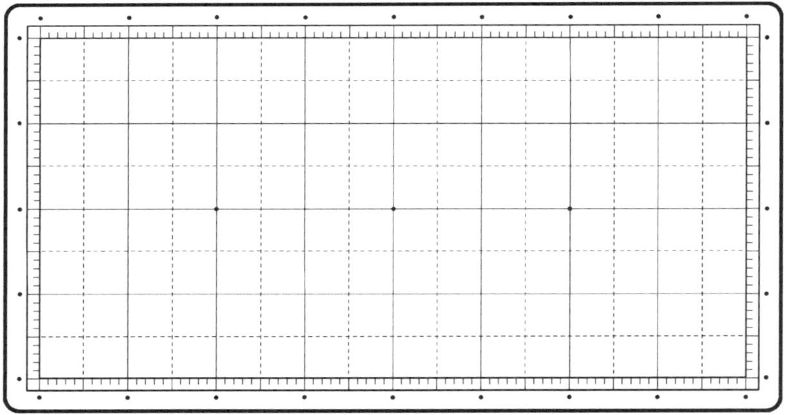

Point:

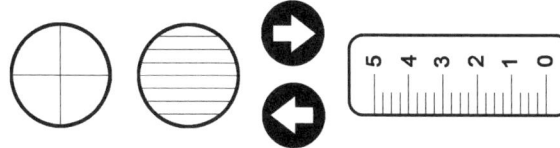

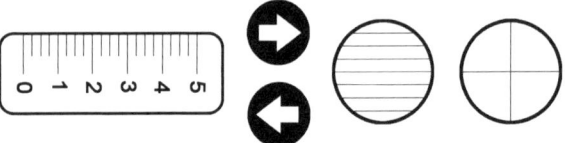

Date:

Position:

Point:

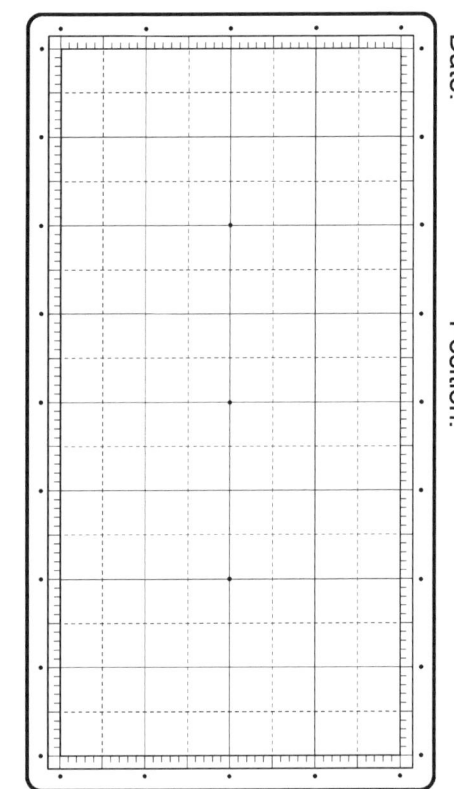

Date: Position:

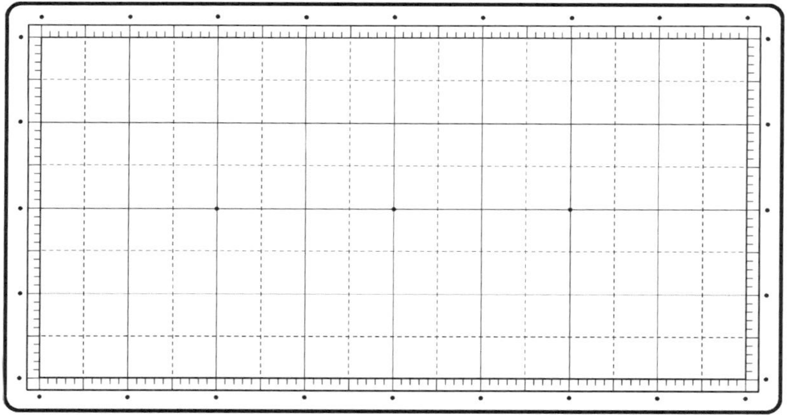

Point:

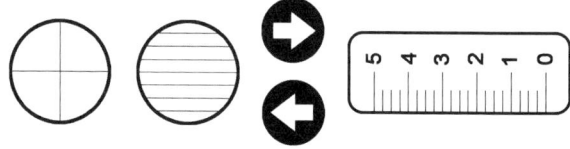

Date: Position:

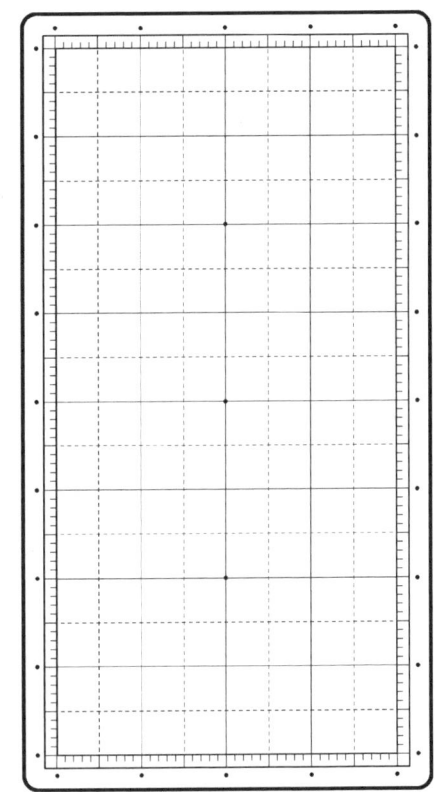

Point:

Date: Position:

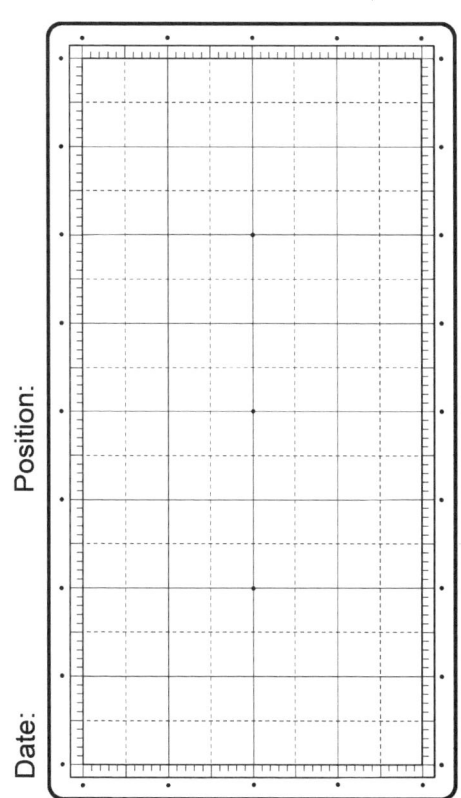

Point:

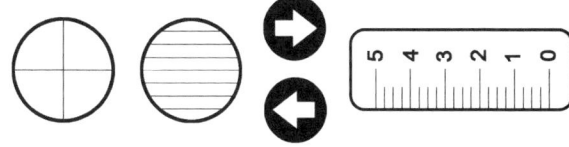

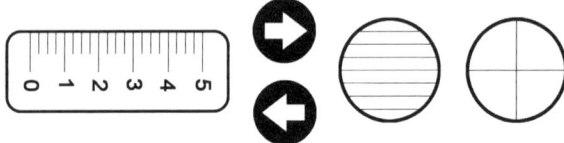

Point:

Date: Position:

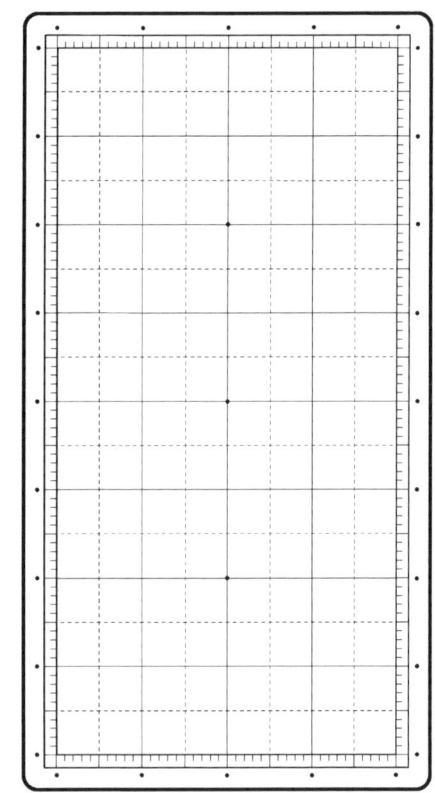

Date: Position:

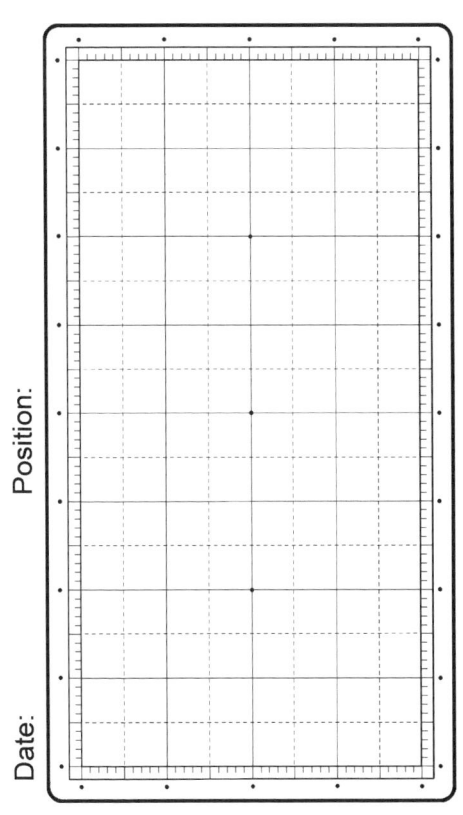

Point:

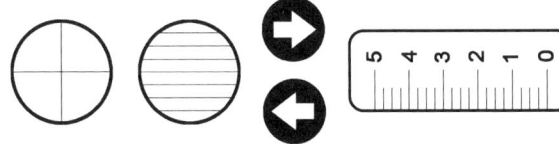

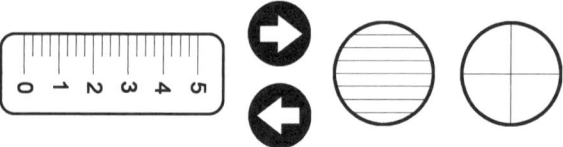

Date:

Position:

Point:

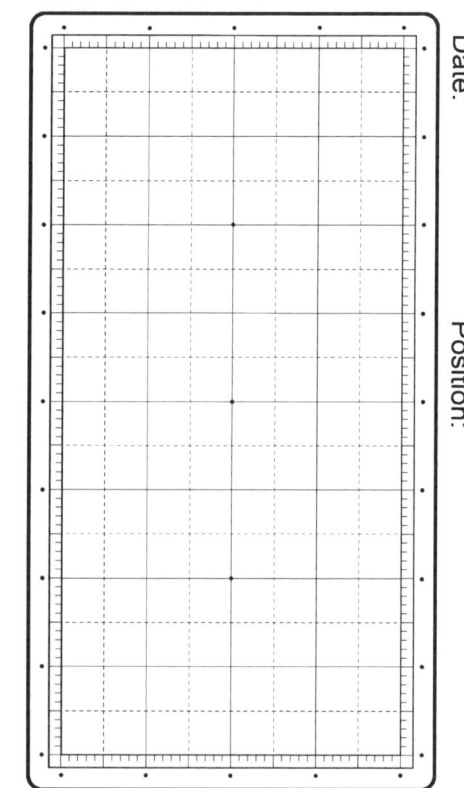

Date: Position:

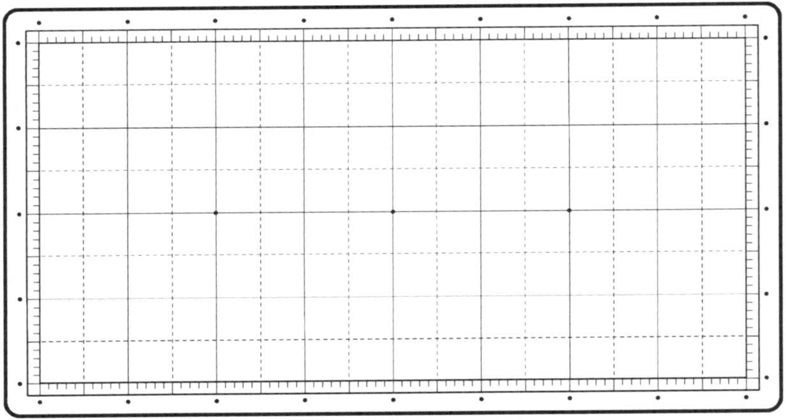

Point:

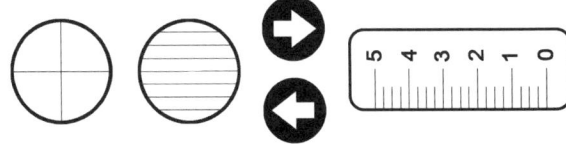

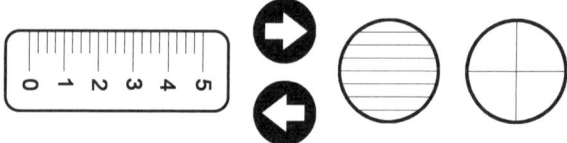

Date:

Position:

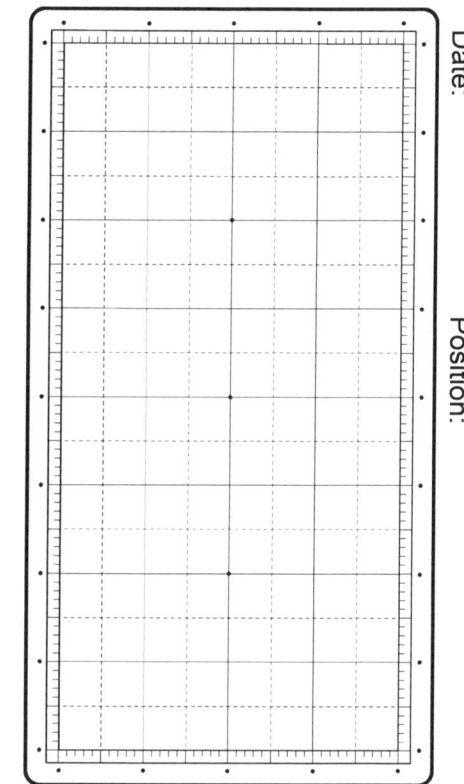

Point:

Date: Position:

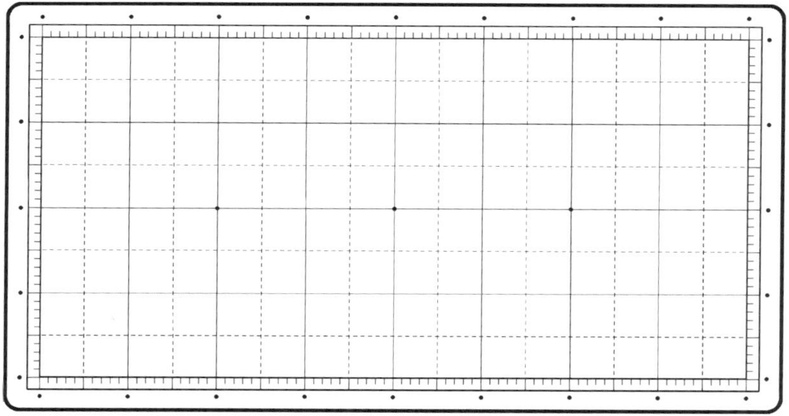

Point:

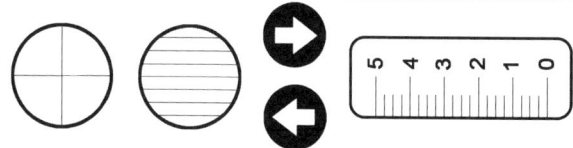

Date:

Position:

Point:

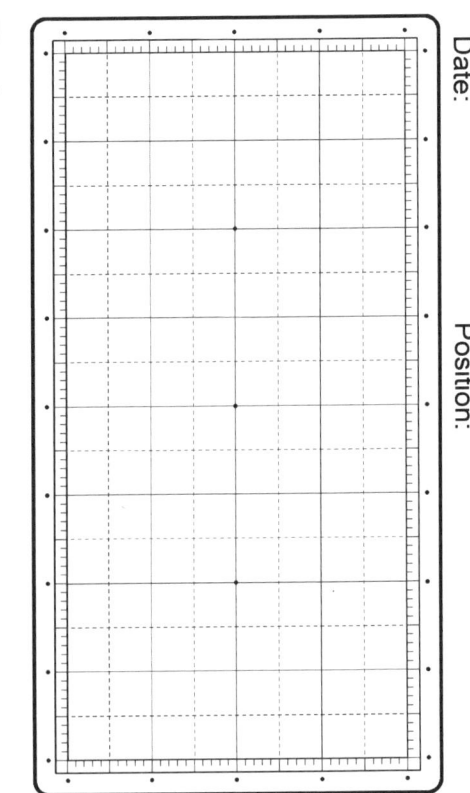

Date:

Position:

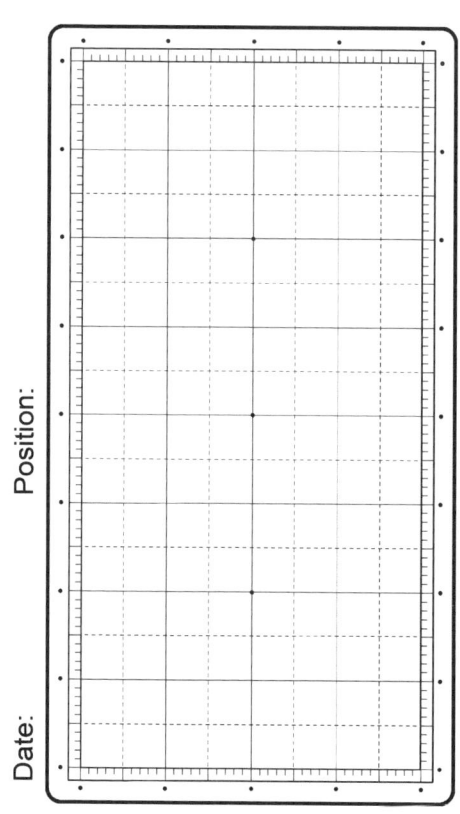

Point:

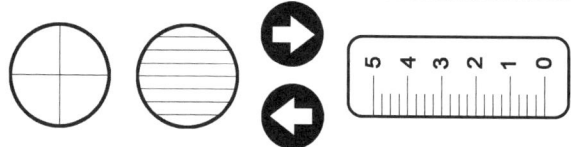

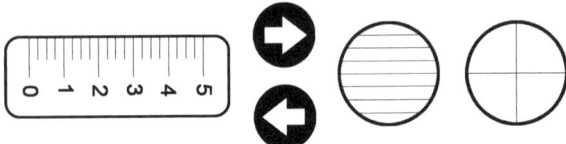

Date: Position:

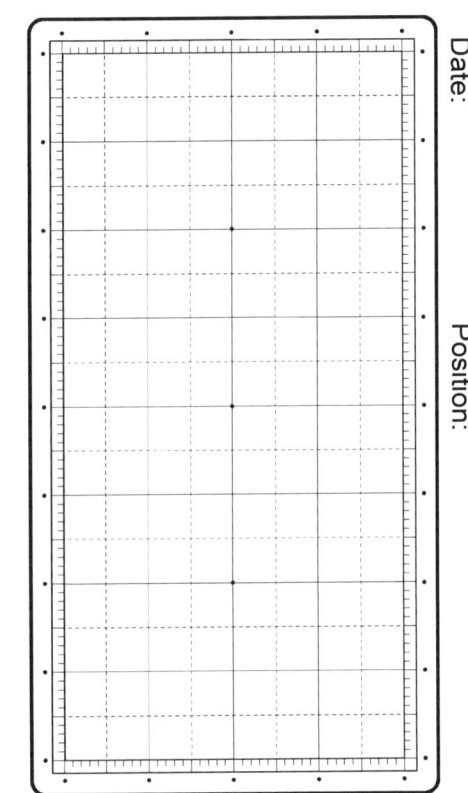

Point:

Date: Position:

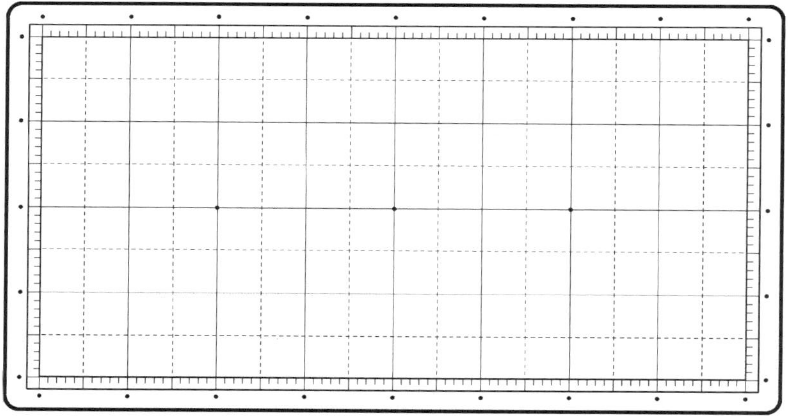

Point:

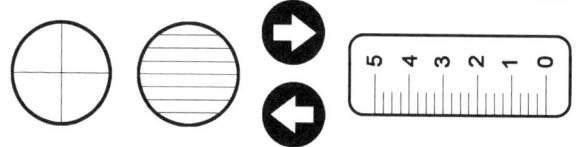

Date: Position:

Point:

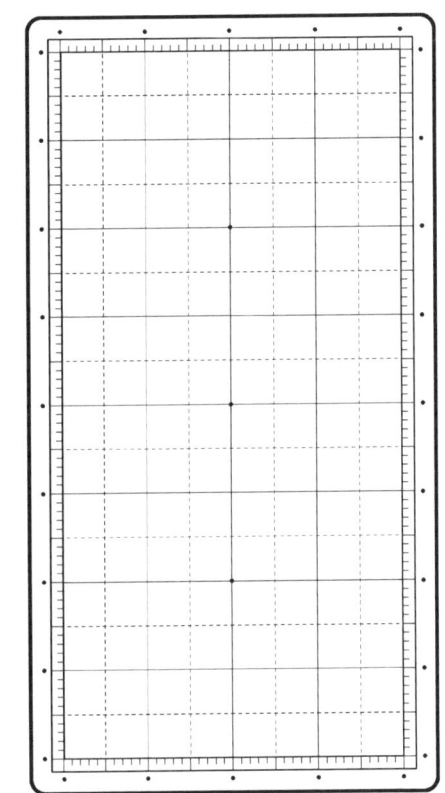

Date: Position:

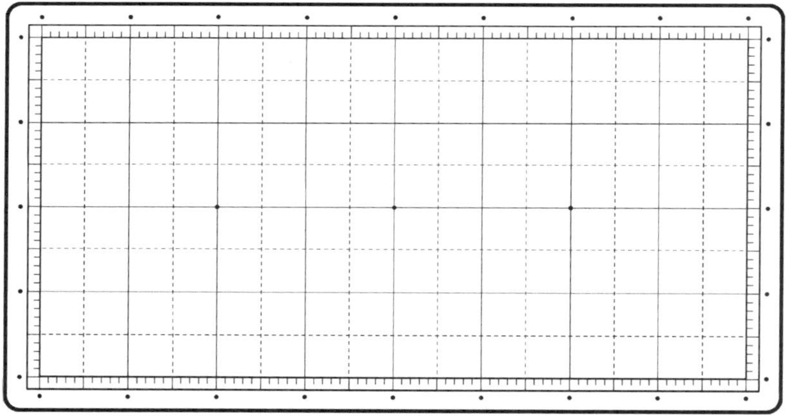

Point:

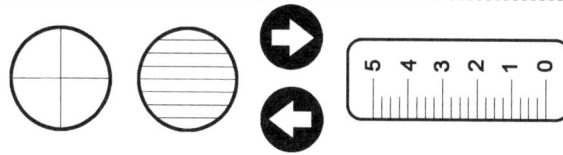

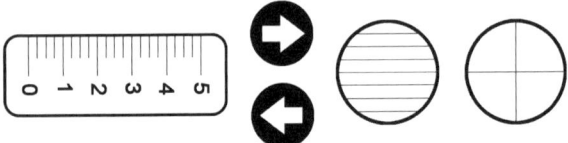

Date: Position:

Point:

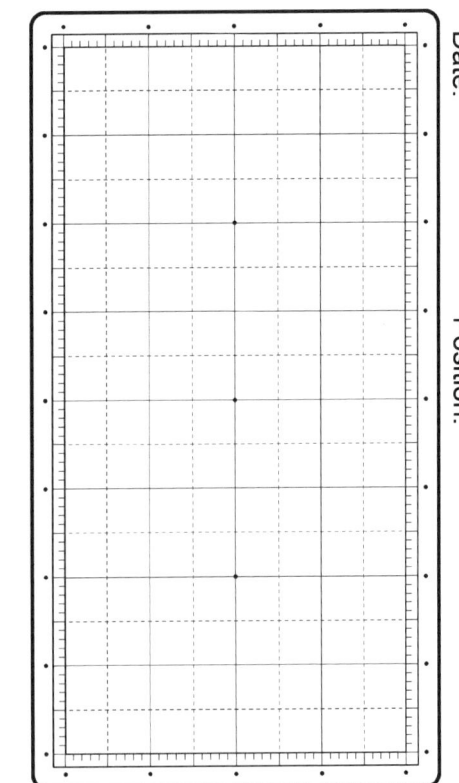

Date:

Position:

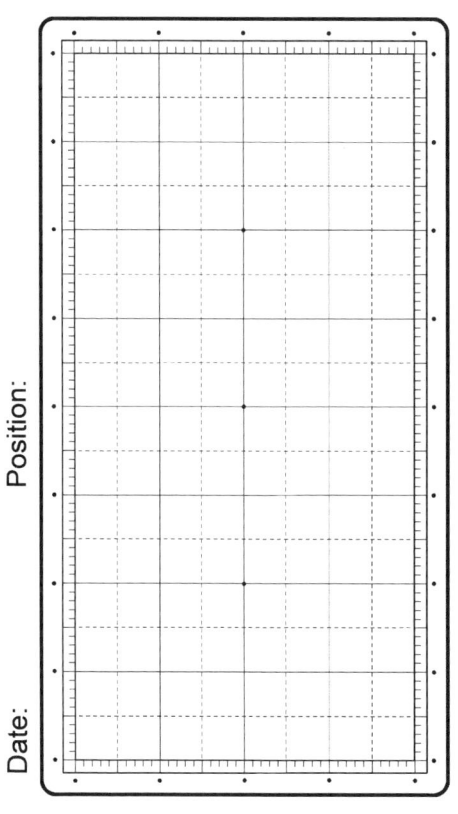

Point:

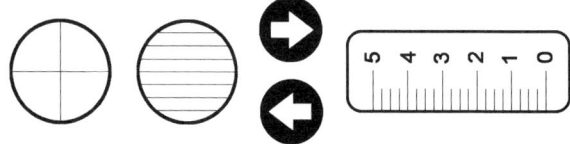

Date: Position:

Point:

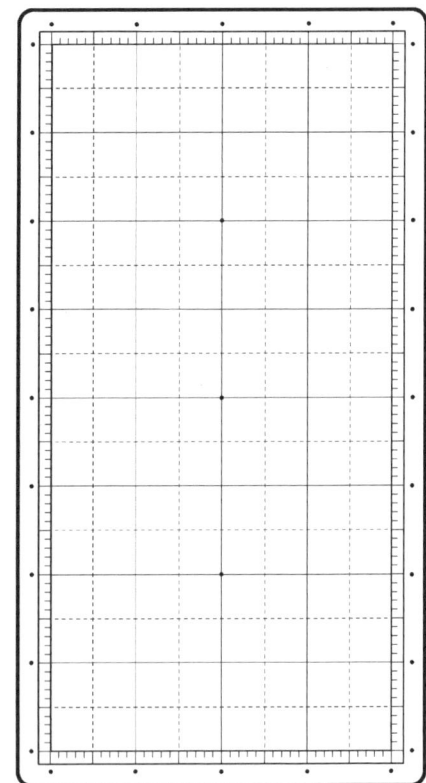

Date: Position:

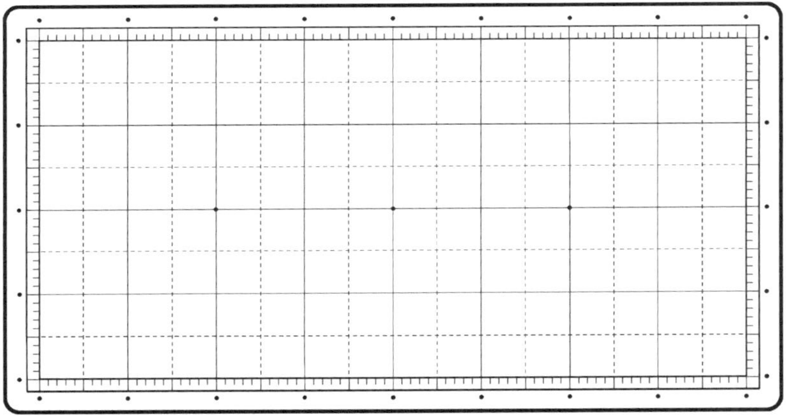

Point:

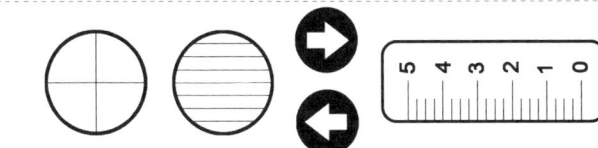

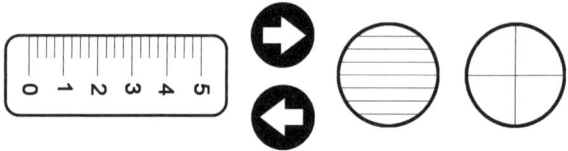

Date:

Position:

Point:

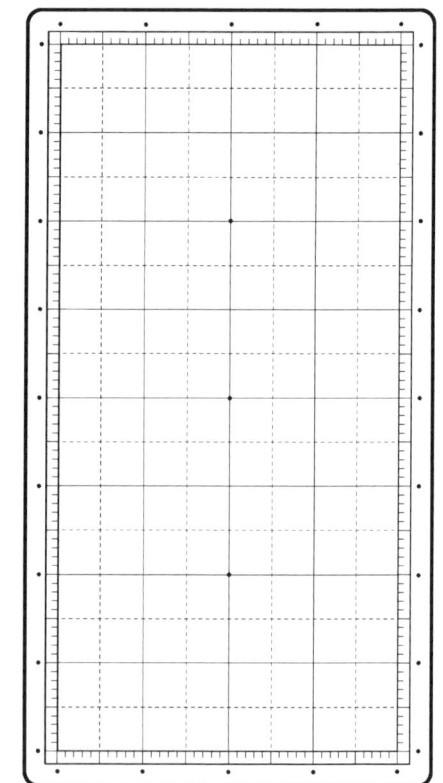

Date: Position:

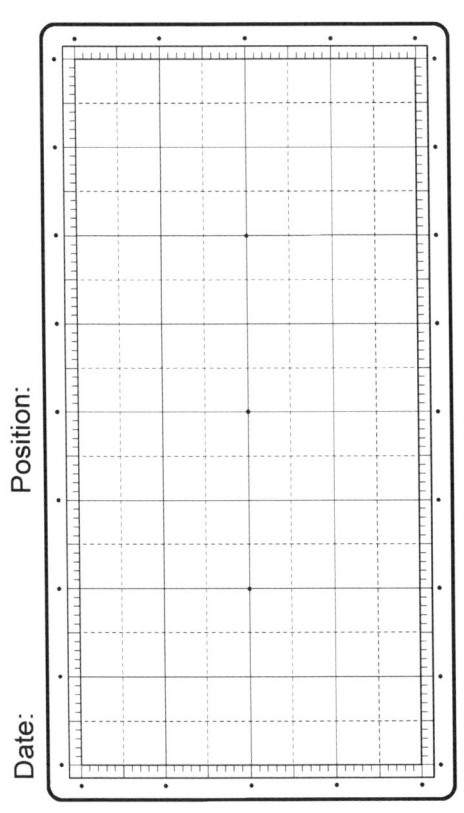

Point:

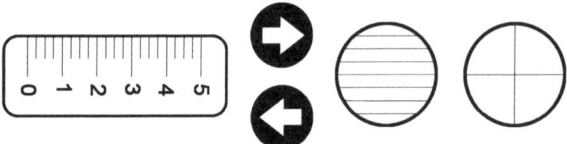

Point:

Date:

Position:

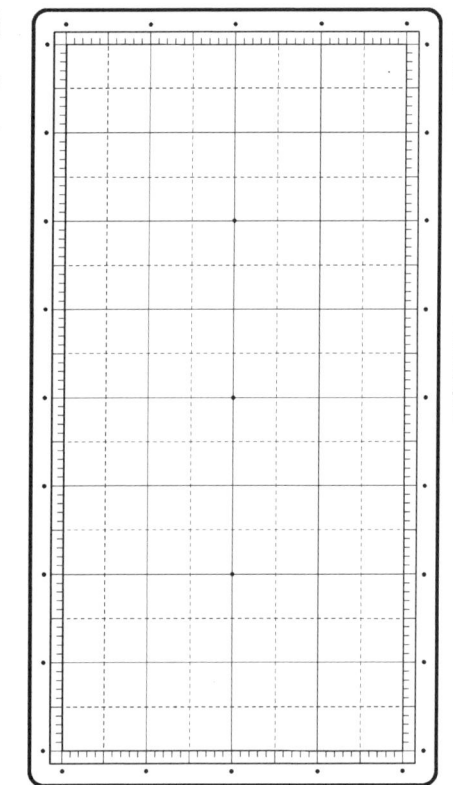

Date: Position:

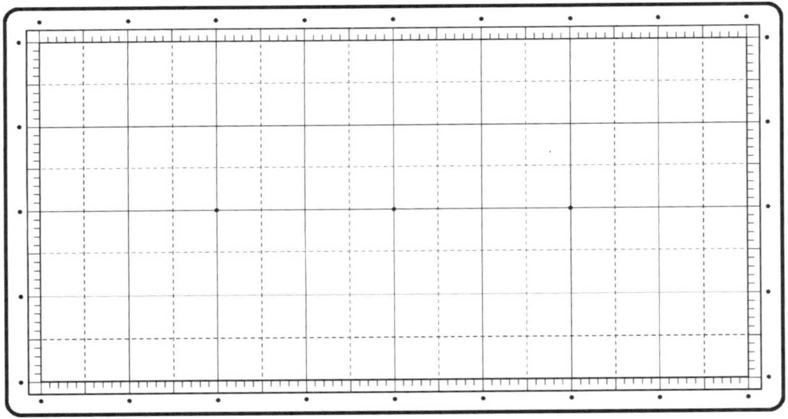

Point:

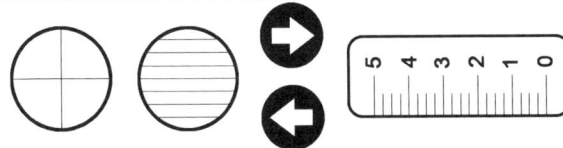

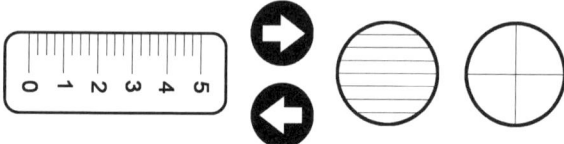

Point:

Date:

Position:

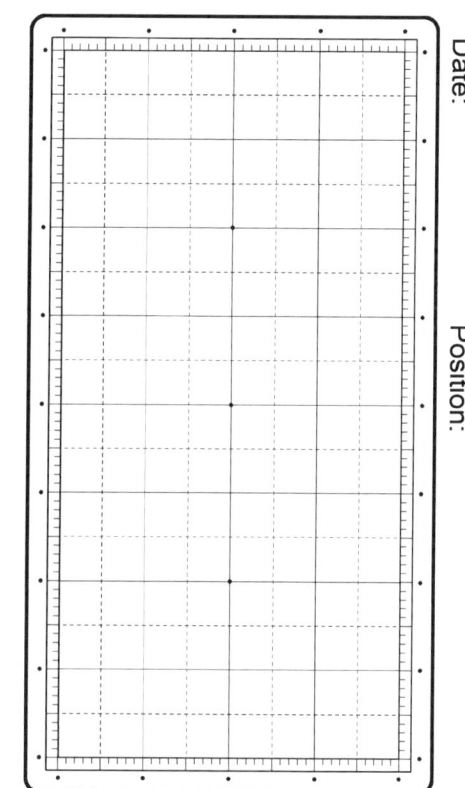

Date: Position:

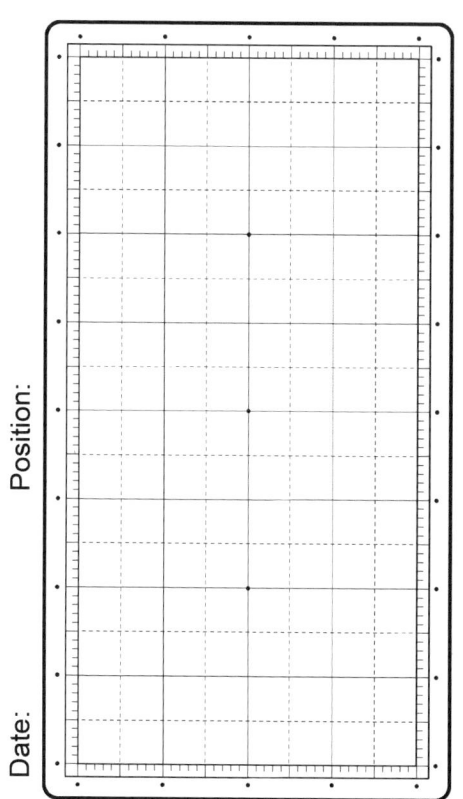

Point:

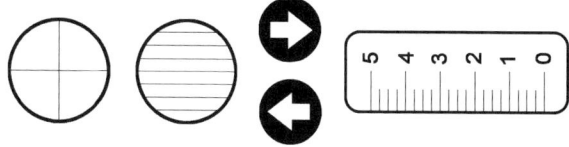

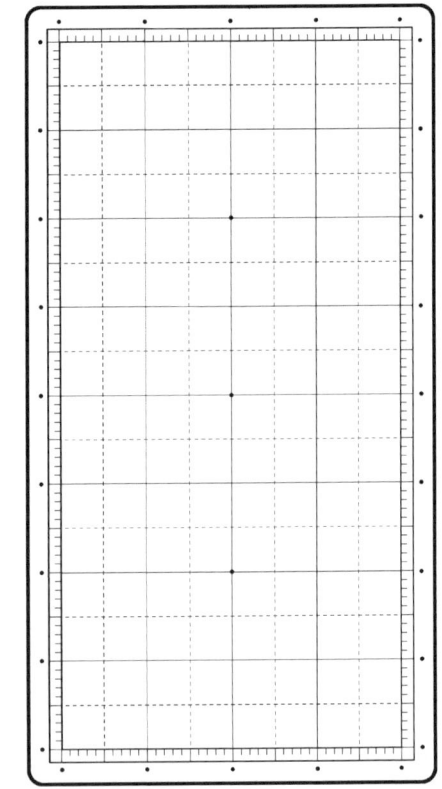

Date:

Position:

Point:

Date: Position:

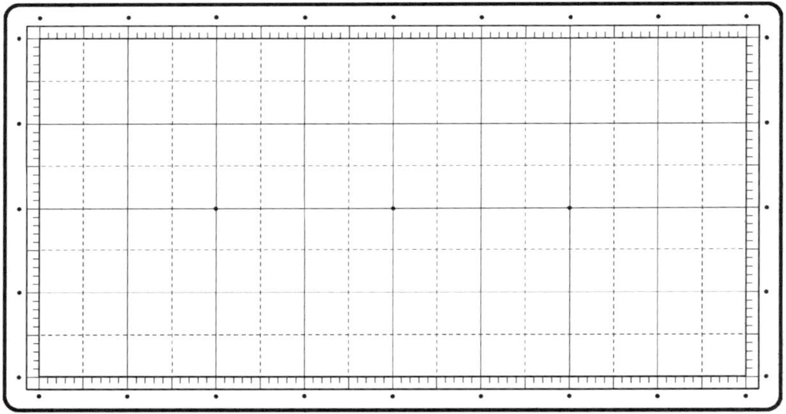

Point:

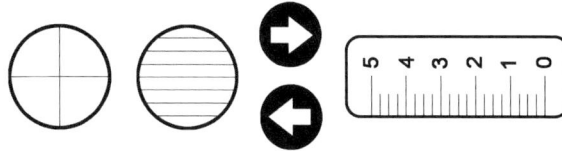

Date: Position:

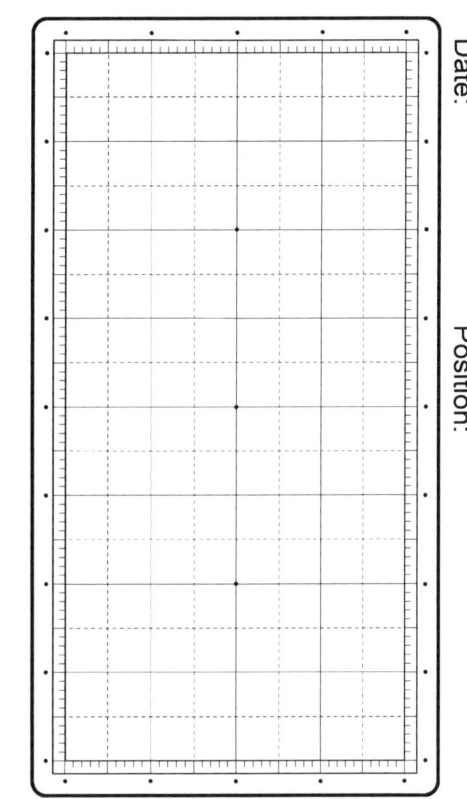

Point:

Date:

Position:

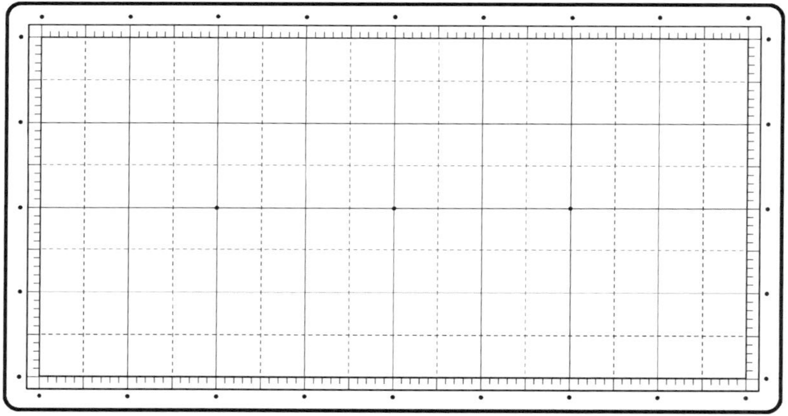

Point:

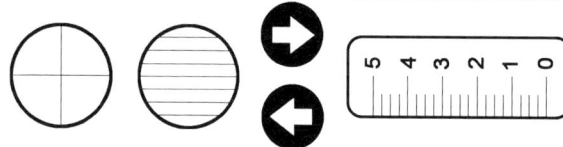

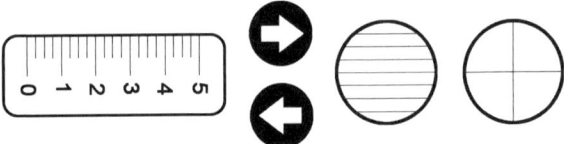

Point:

Date: Position:

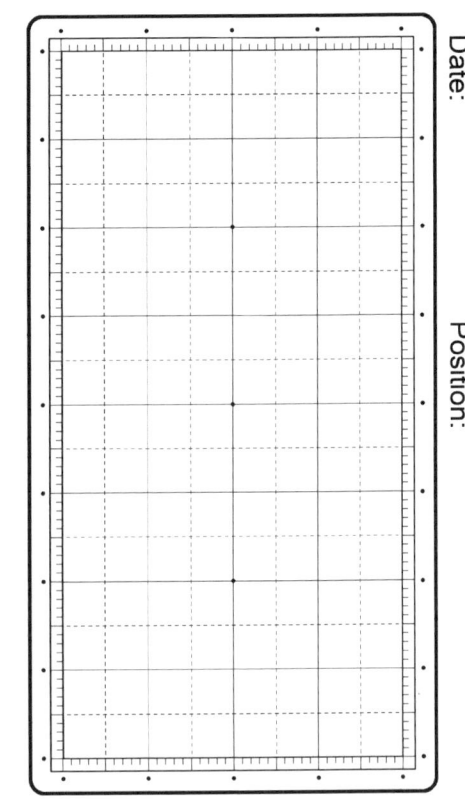

Date: Position:

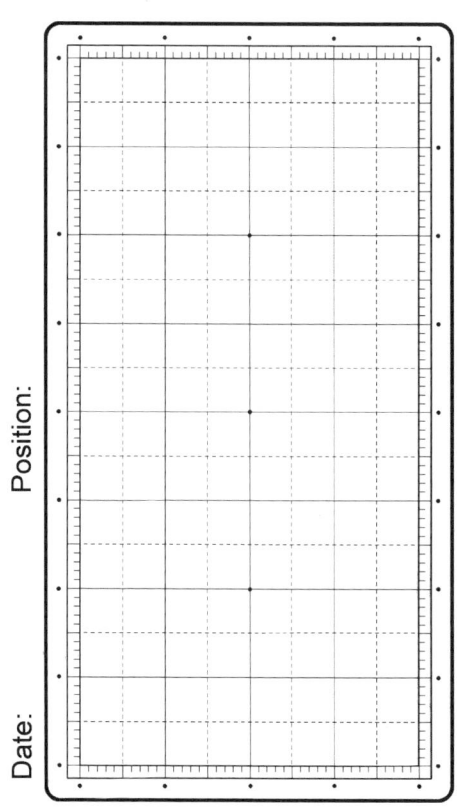

Point:

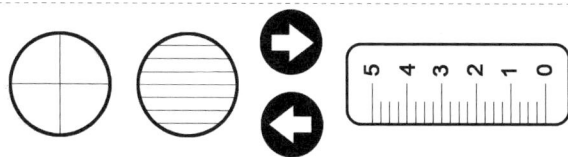

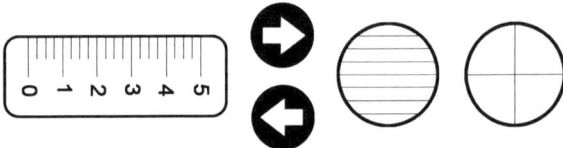

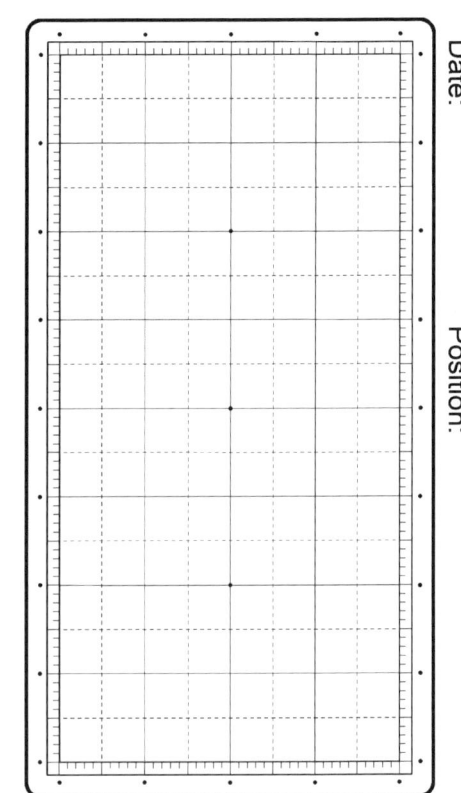

Date: Position:

Point:

Date: Position:

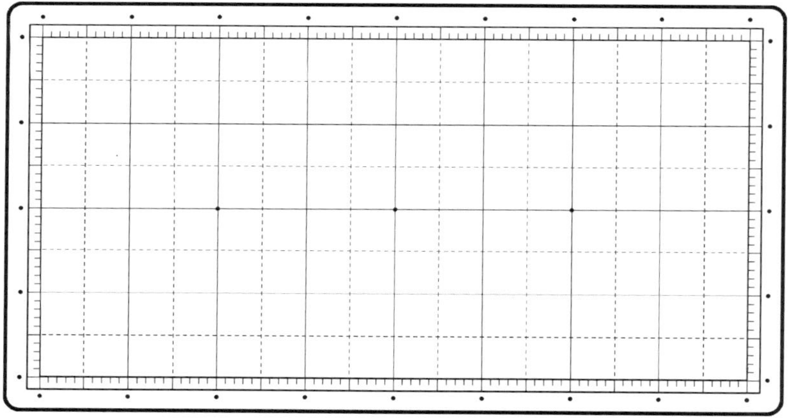

Point:

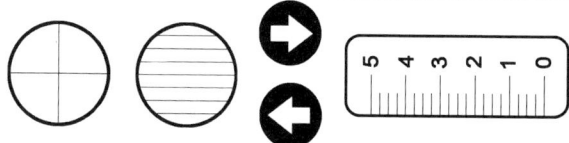

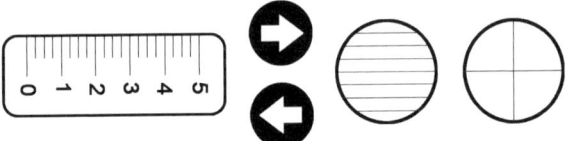

Date: Position:

Point:

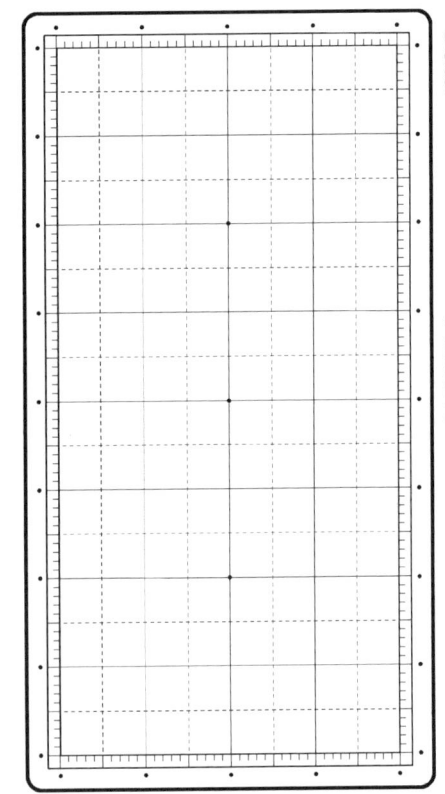

Date:

Position:

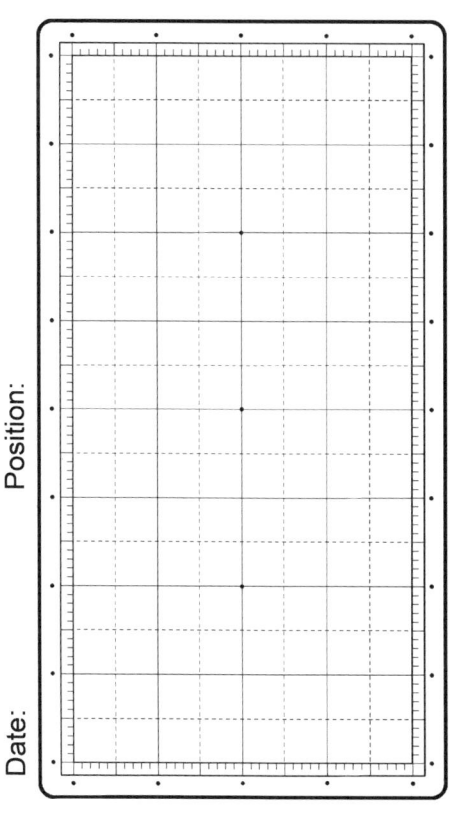

Point:

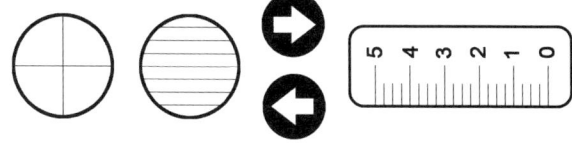

Date: Position:

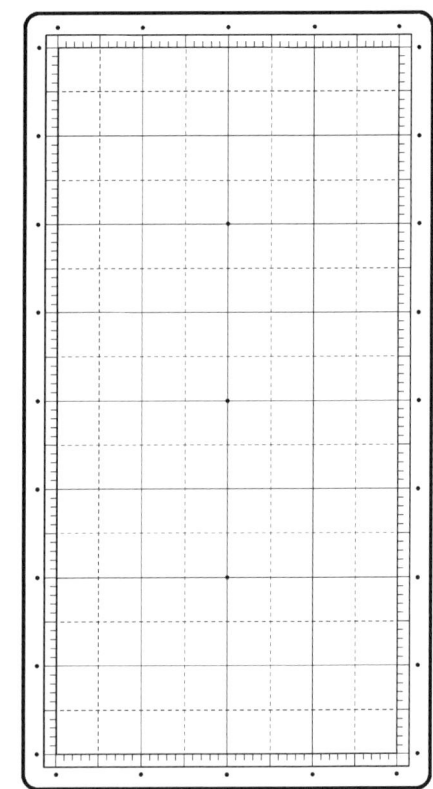

Point:

Date:

Position:

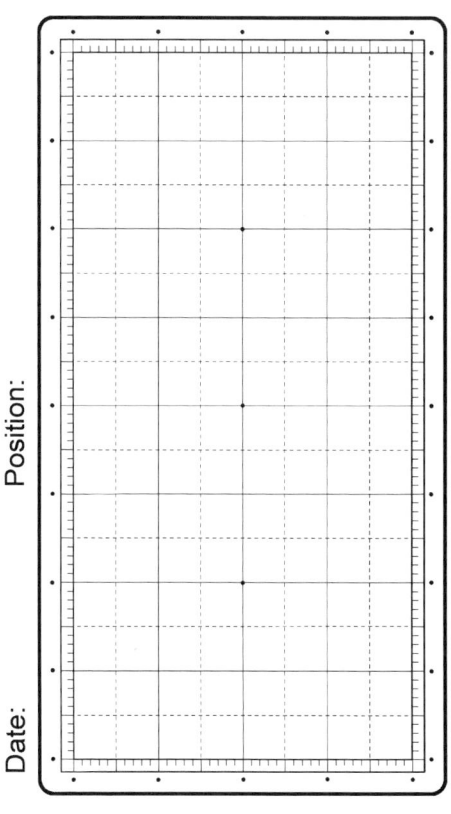

Point:

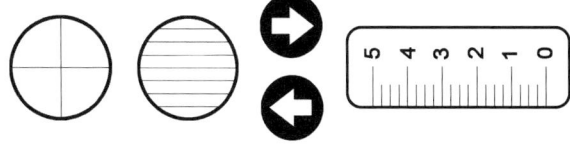

Date:

Position:

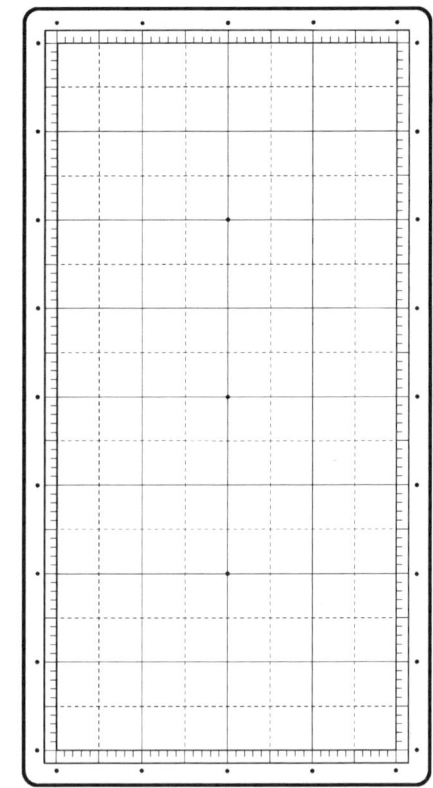

Point:

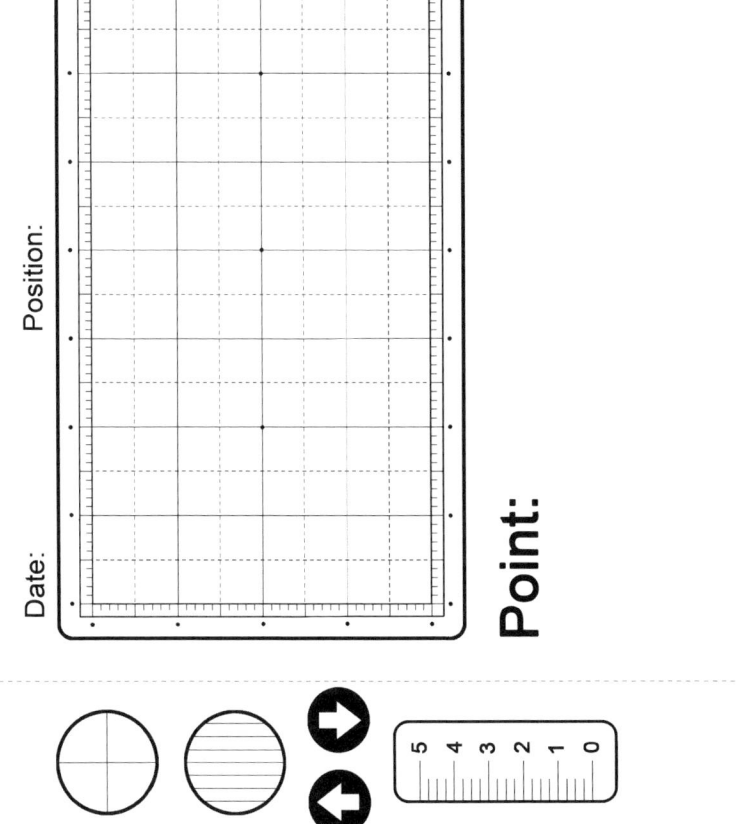

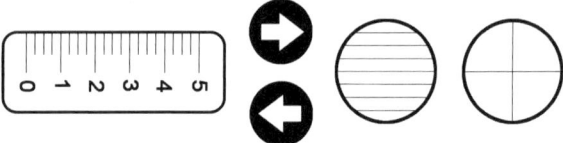

Date:

Position:

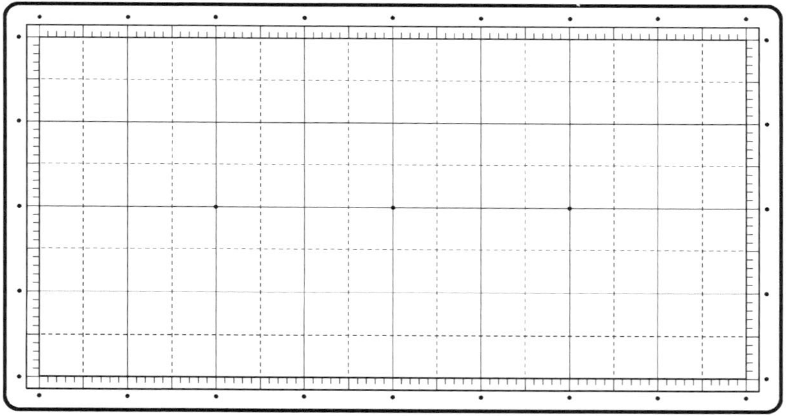

Point:

Date: Position:

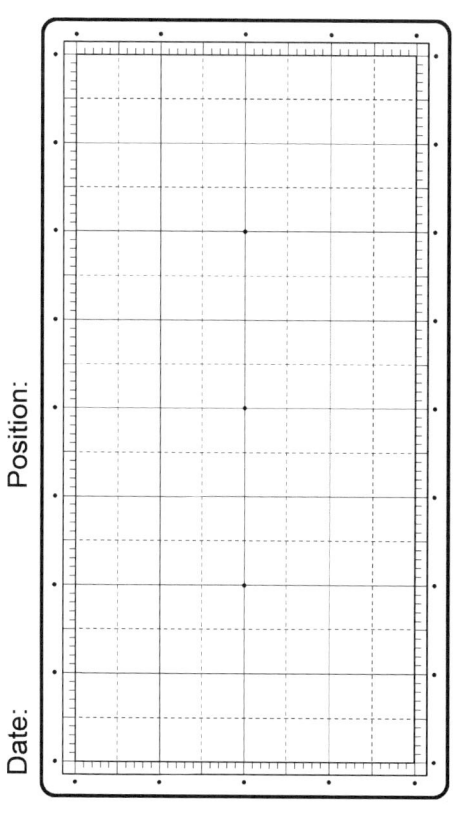

Point:

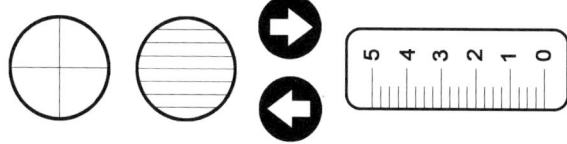

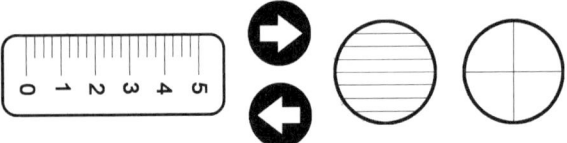

Date: Position:

Point:

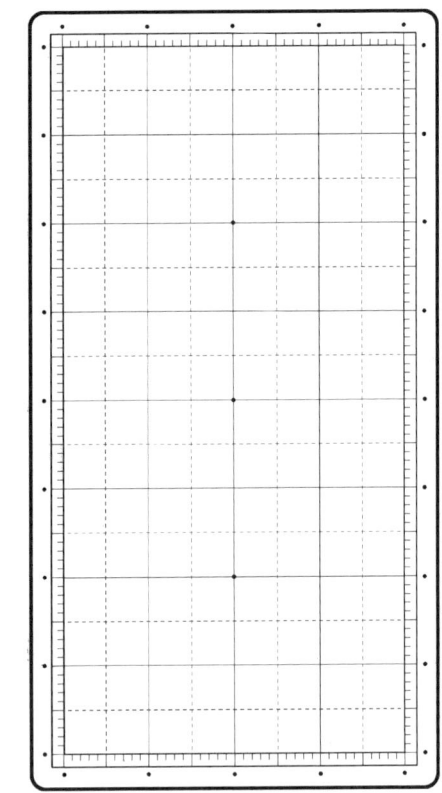

Date: Position:

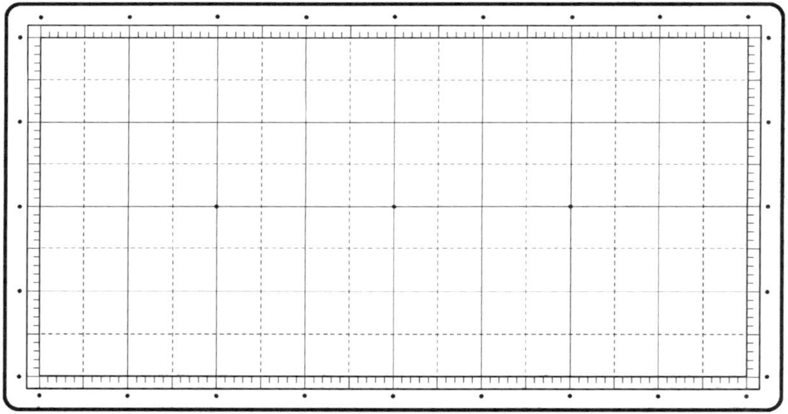

Point:

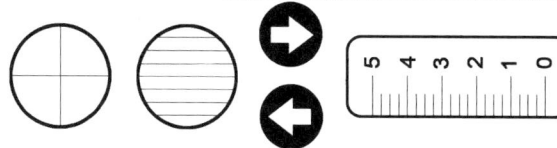

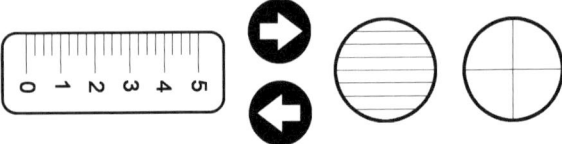

Date: Position:

Point:

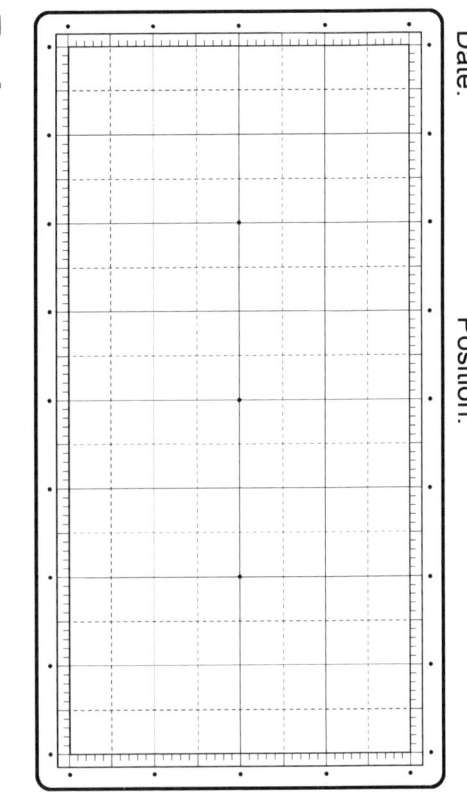

Date: Position:

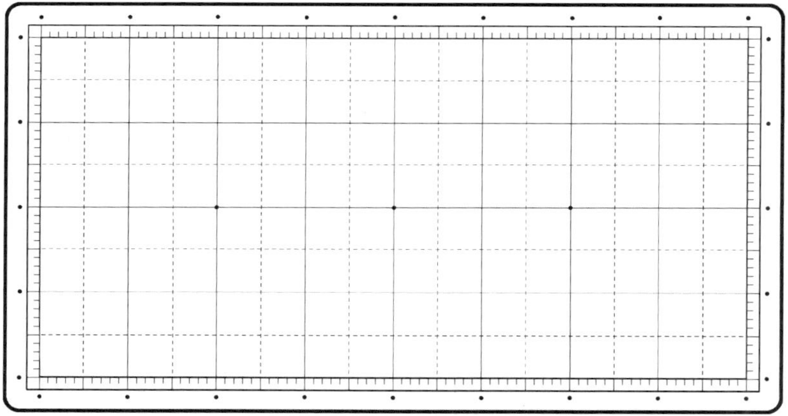

Point:

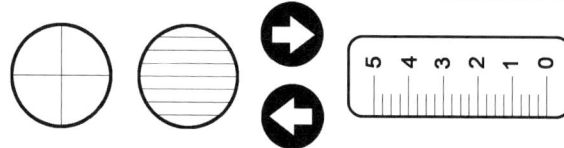

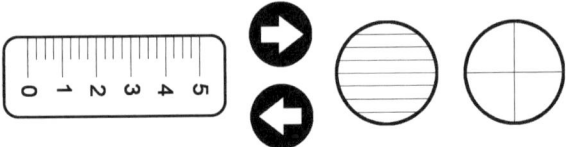

Date:

Position:

Point:

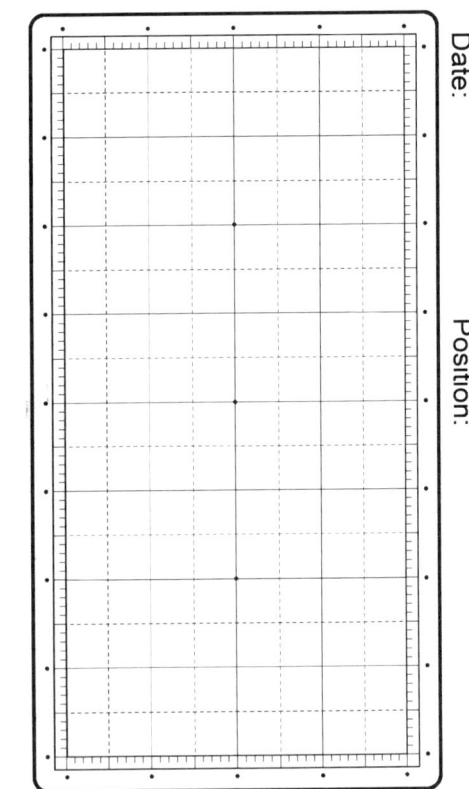

Date: Position:

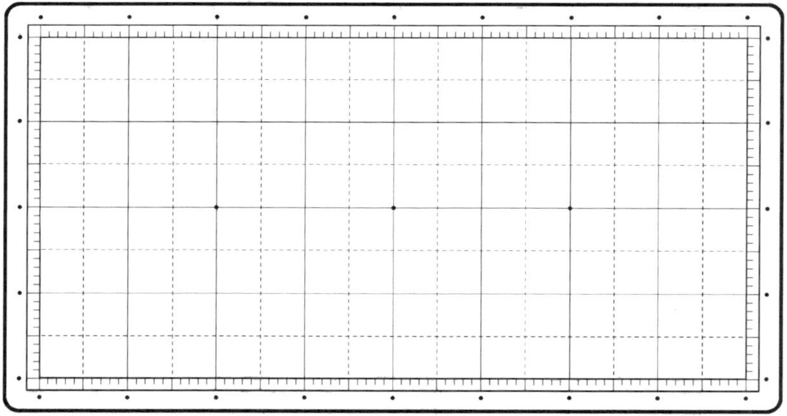

Point:

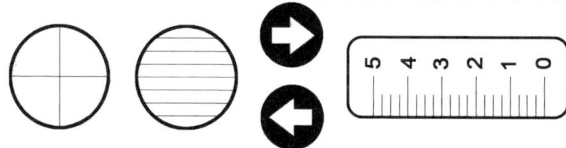

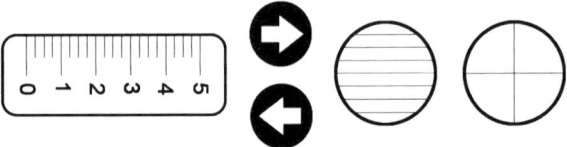

Date: Position:

Point:

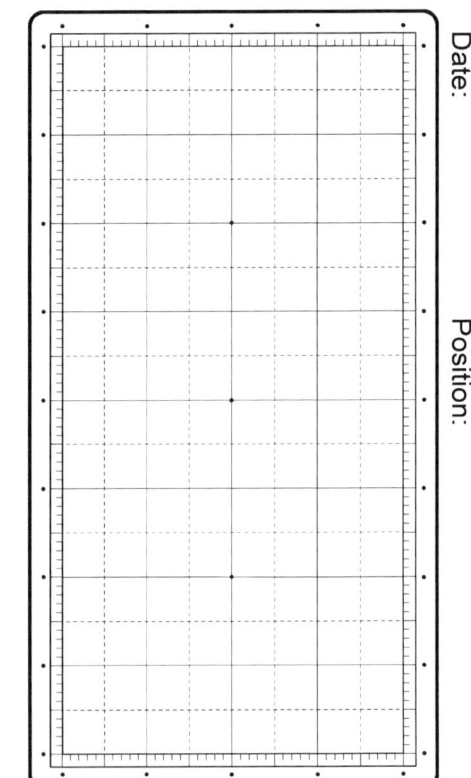

Date: Position:

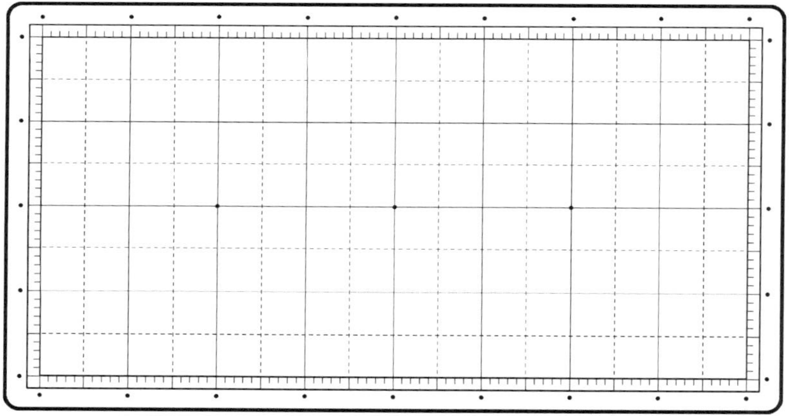

Point:

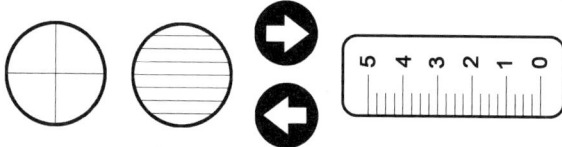

Date: Position:

Point:

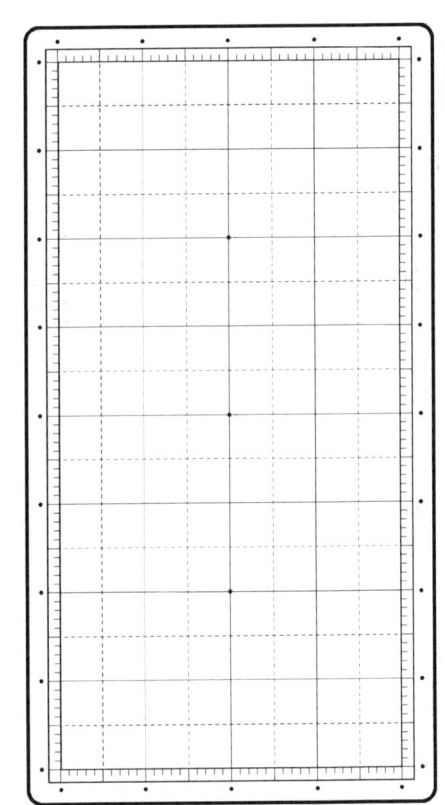

Date:

Position:

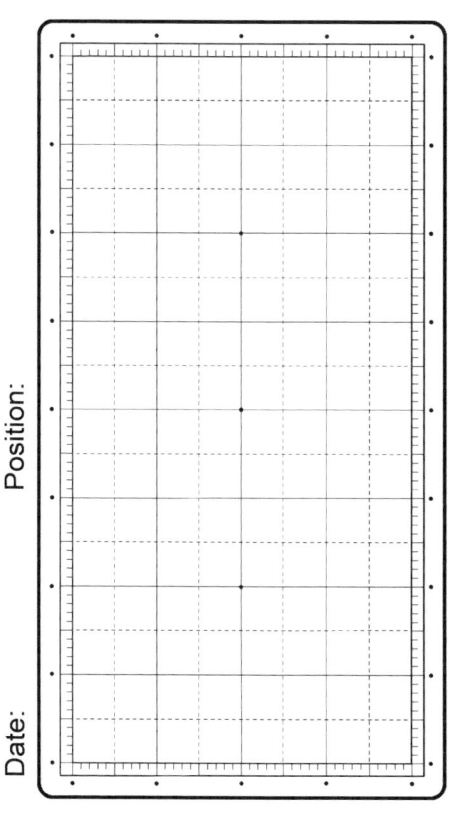

Point:

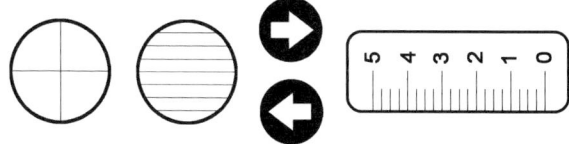

Date: Position:

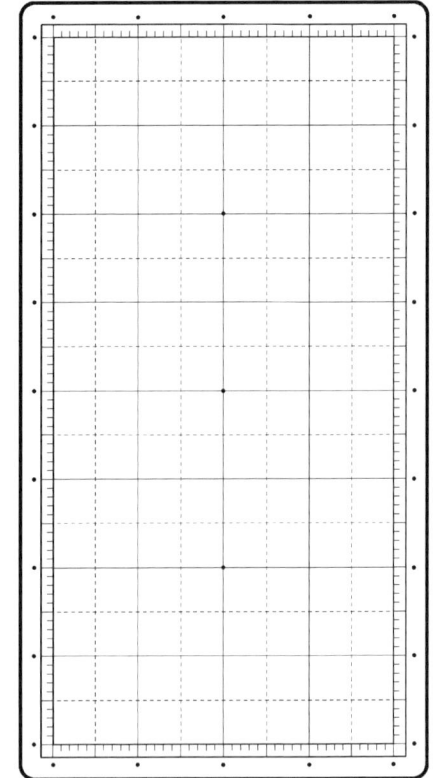

Point:

Date: Position:

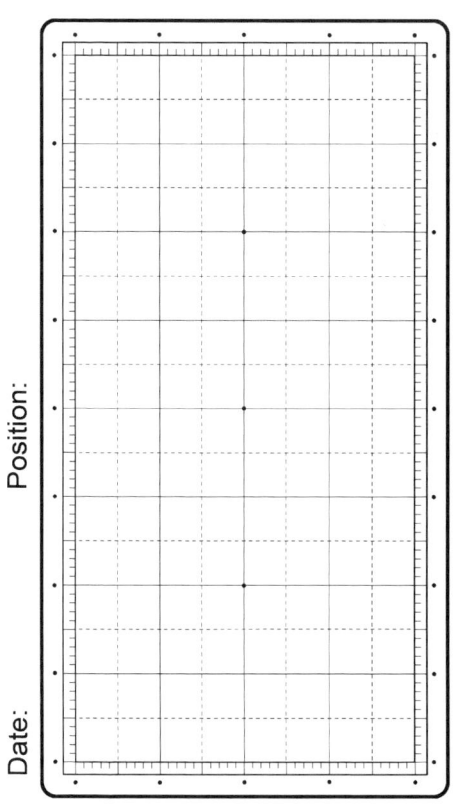

Point:

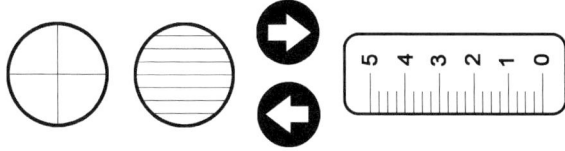

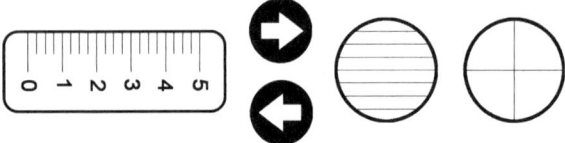

Date:

Position:

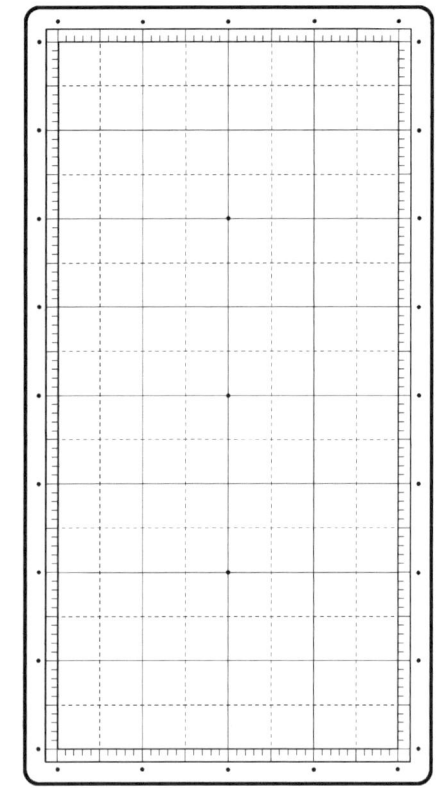

Point:

Date: Position:

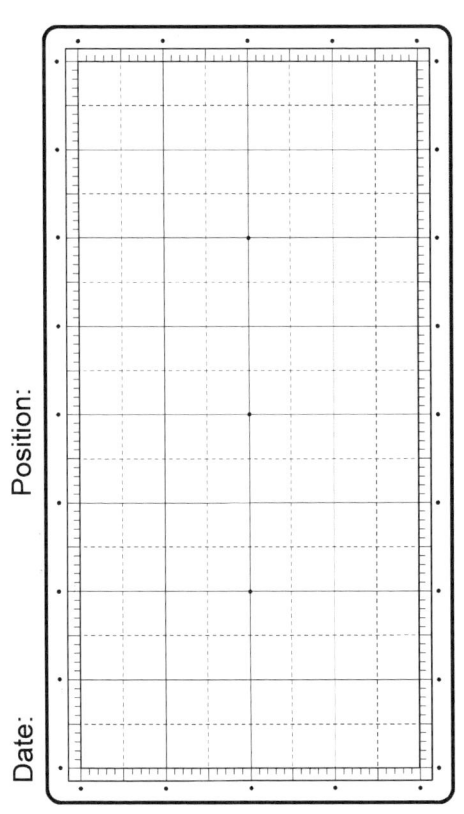

Point:

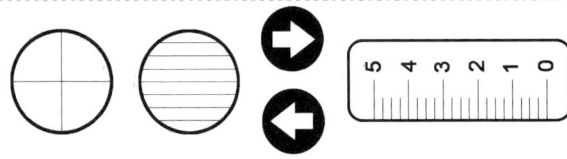

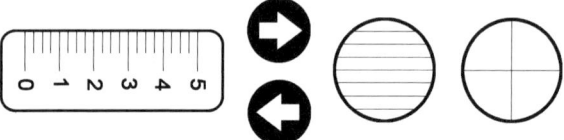

Date: Position:

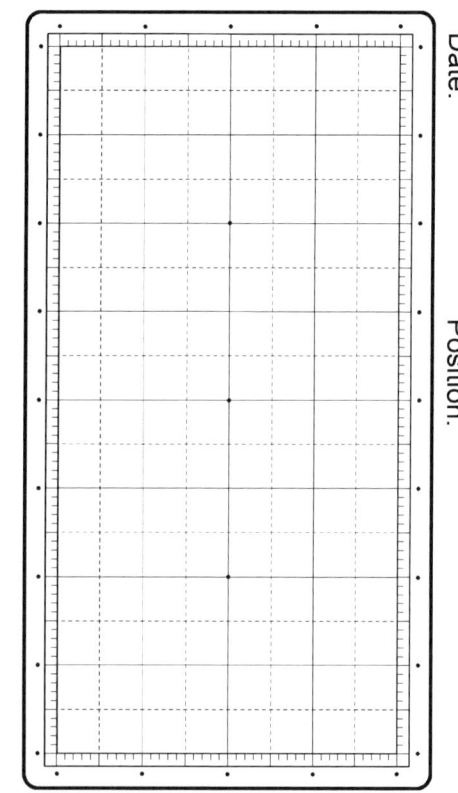

Point:

Date: Position:

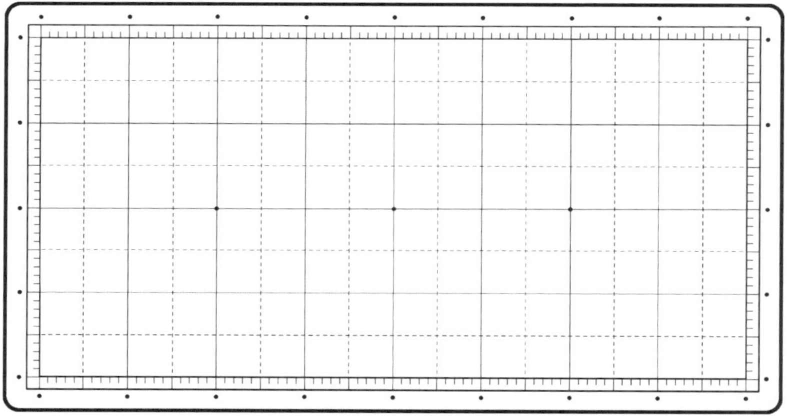

Point:

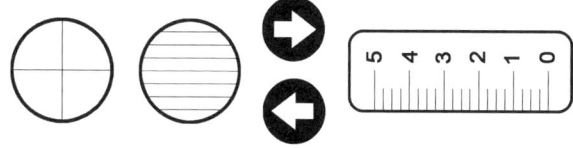

Date: Position:

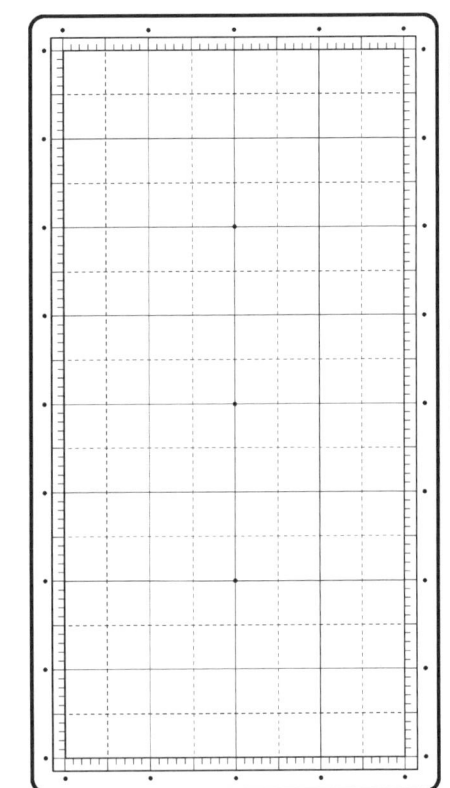

Point:

Date: Position:

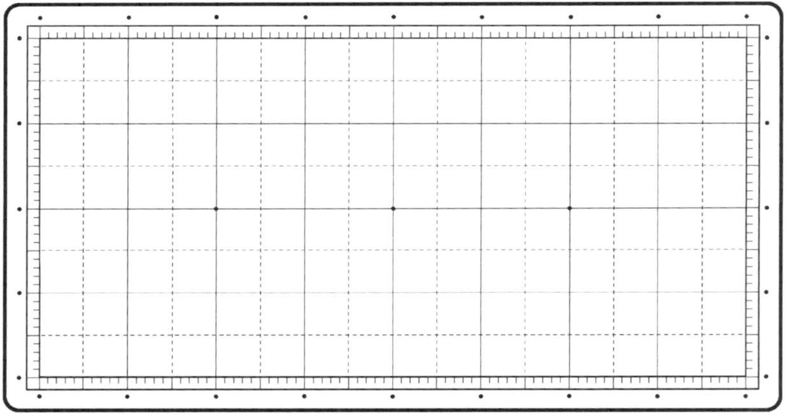

Point:

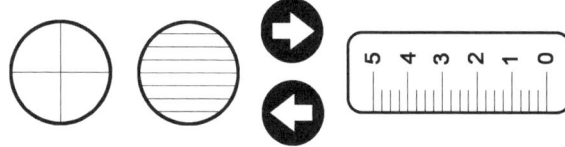

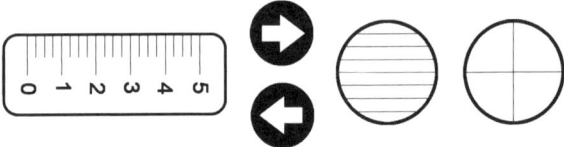

Point:

Date: Position:

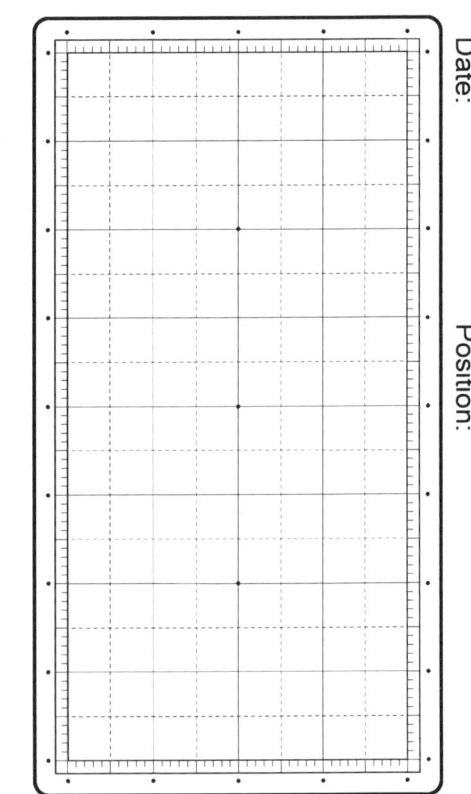

Date: Position:

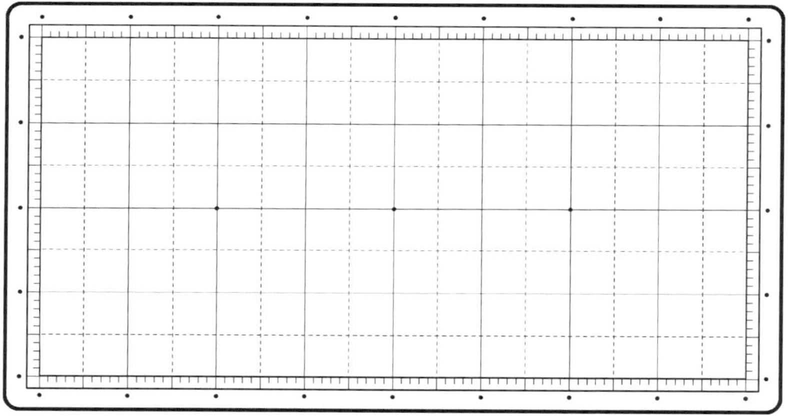

Point:

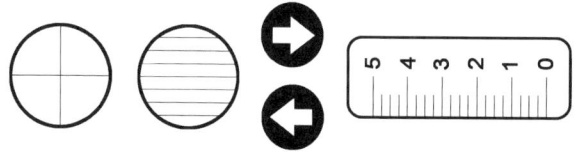

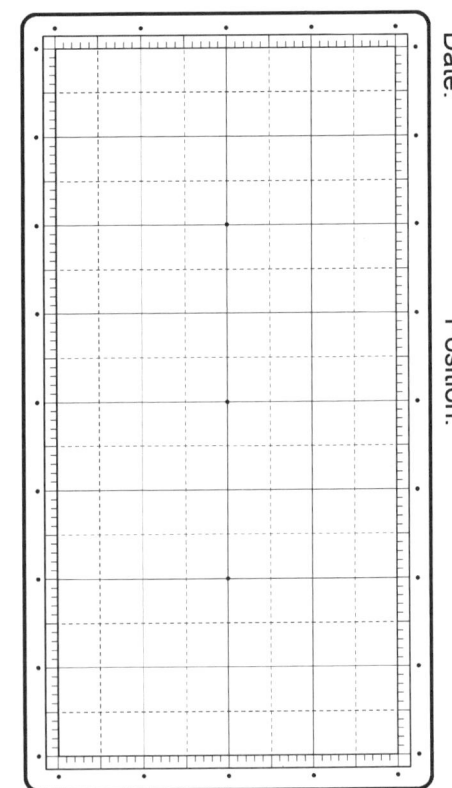

Date:

Position:

Point:

Date: Position:

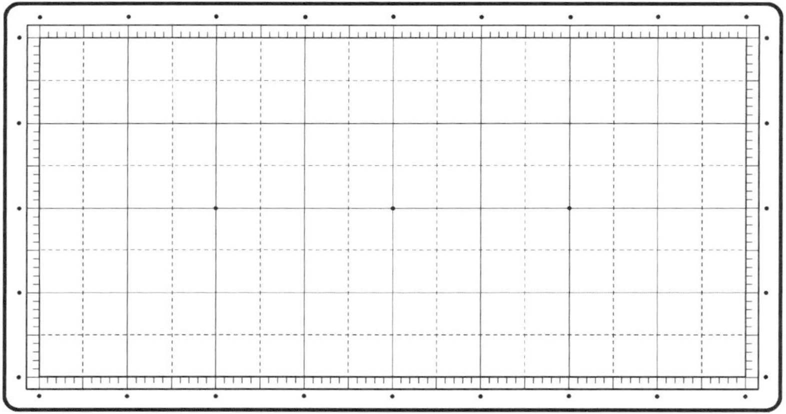

Point:

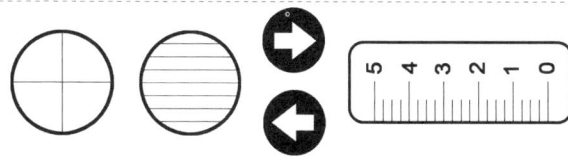

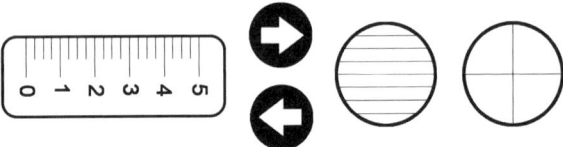

Date: Position:

Point:

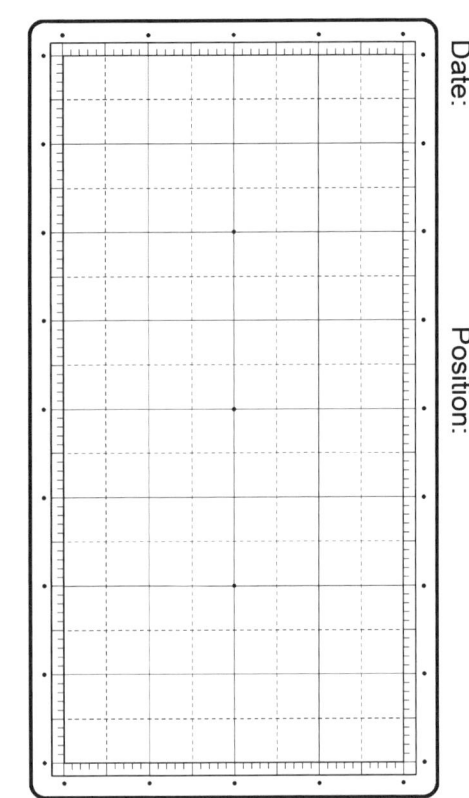

Date: Position:

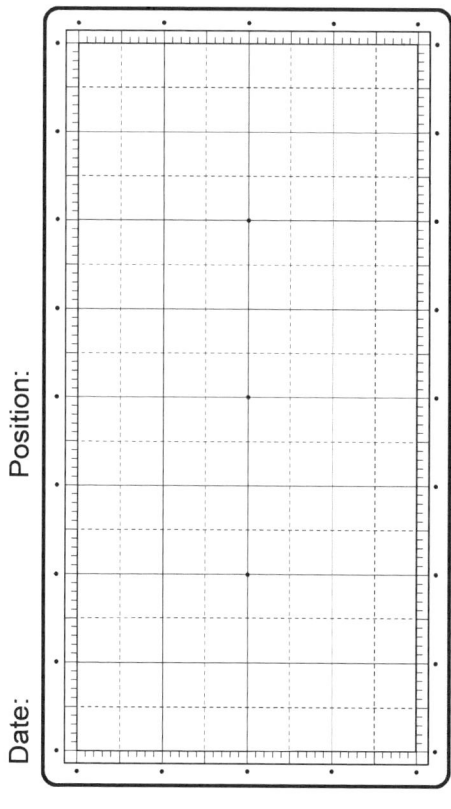

Point:

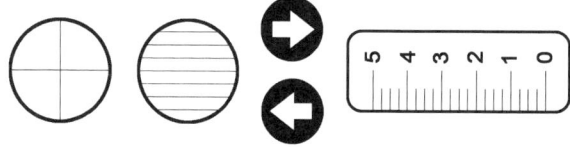

Date: Position:

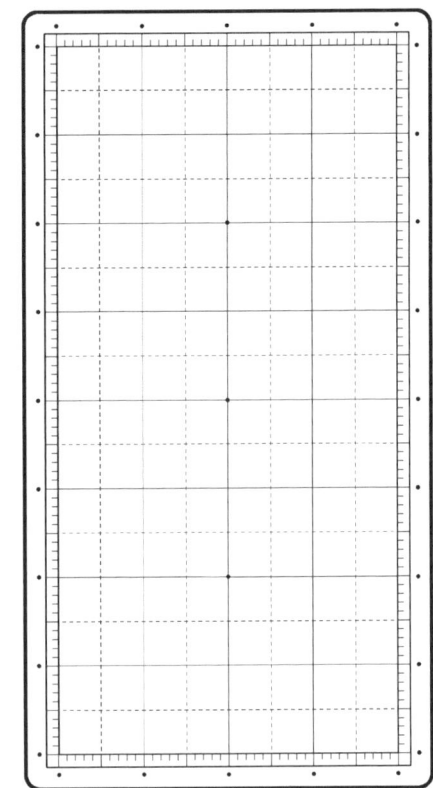

Point:

Date: Position:

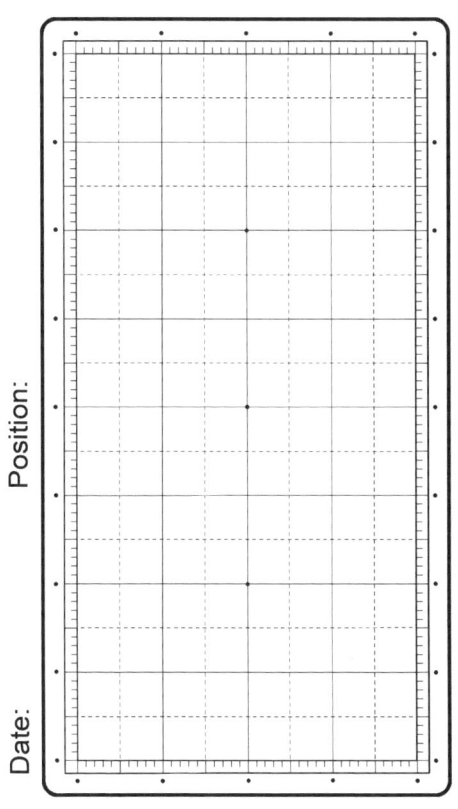

Point:

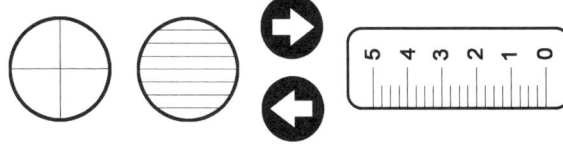

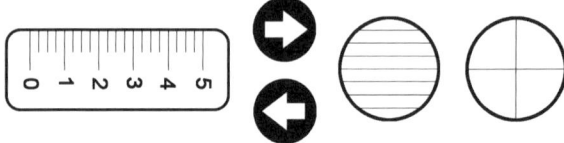

Date: Position:

Point:

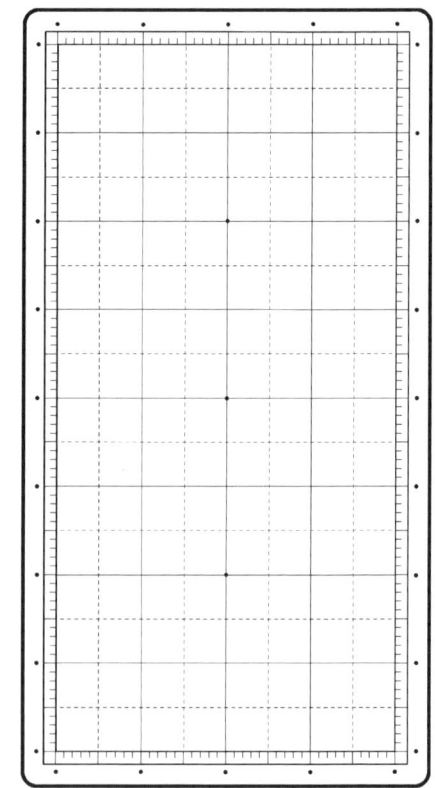

Date: Position:

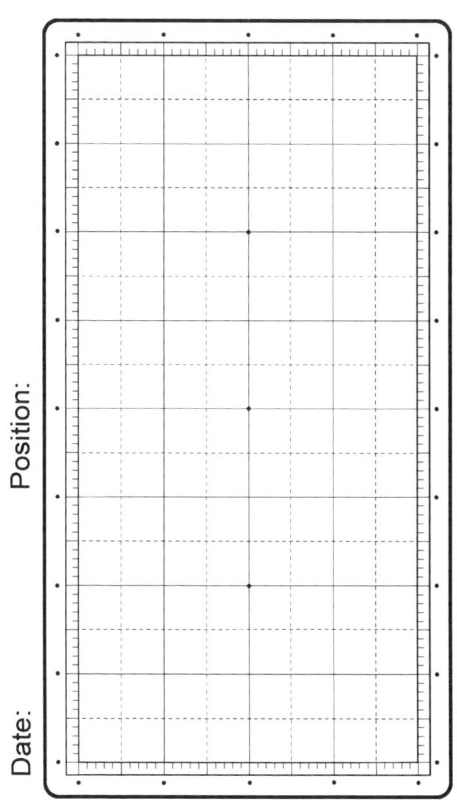

Point:

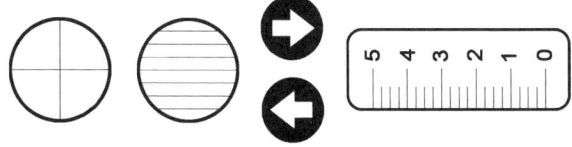

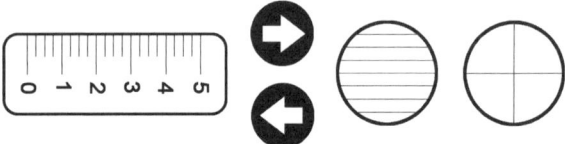

Point:

Date:

Position:

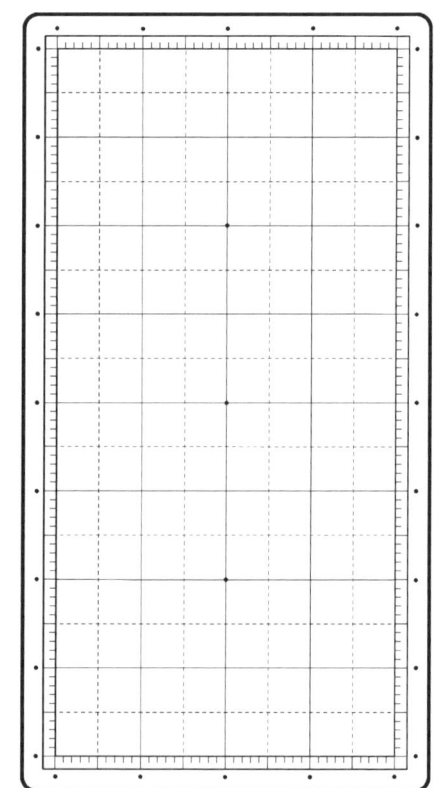

Date: Position:

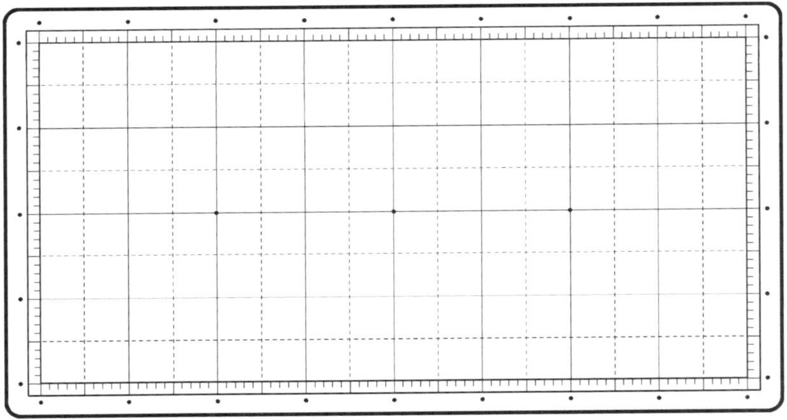

Point:

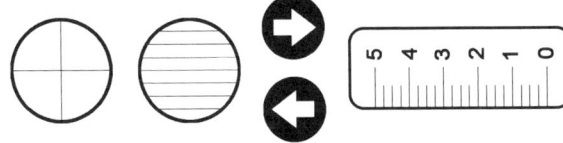

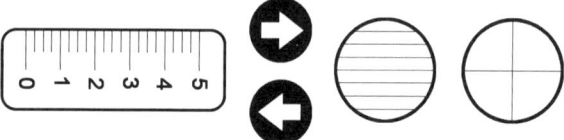

Date:

Position:

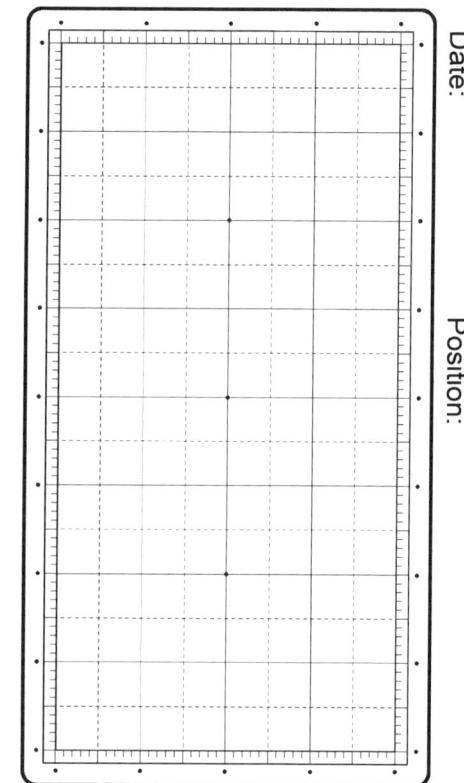

Point:

Date:

Position:

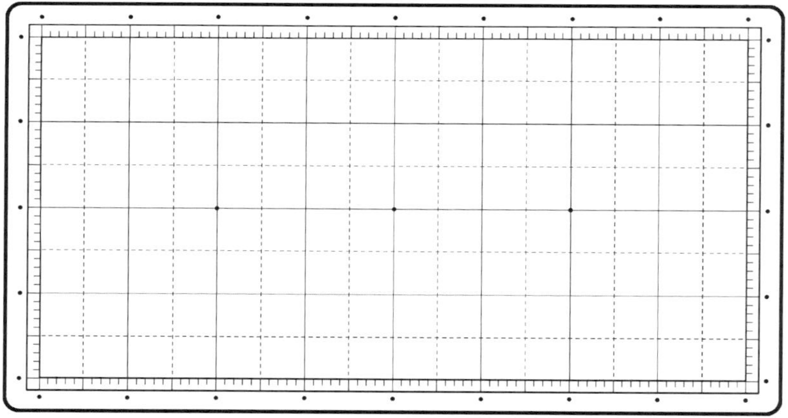

Point:

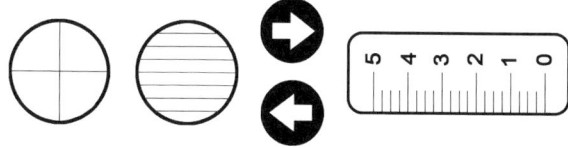

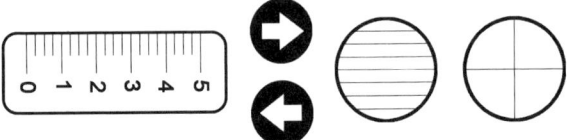

Point:

Date:

Position:

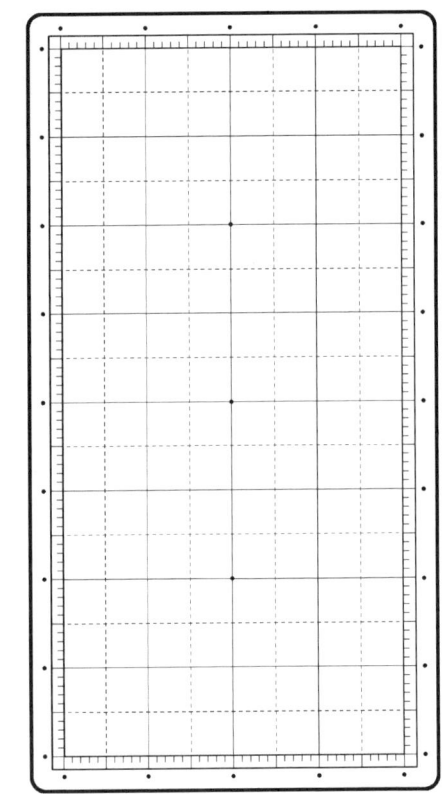

Date: Position:

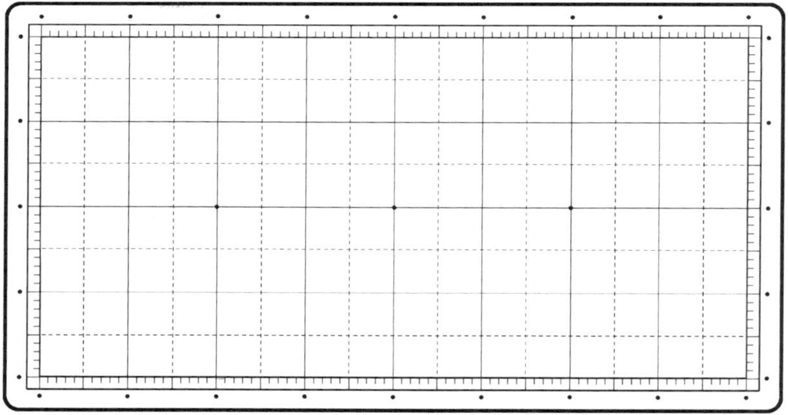

Point:

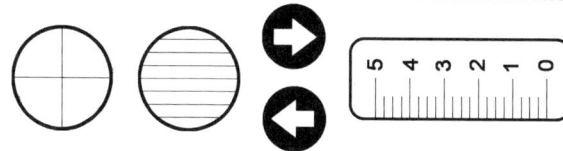

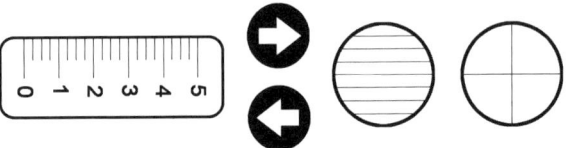

Date: Position:

Point:

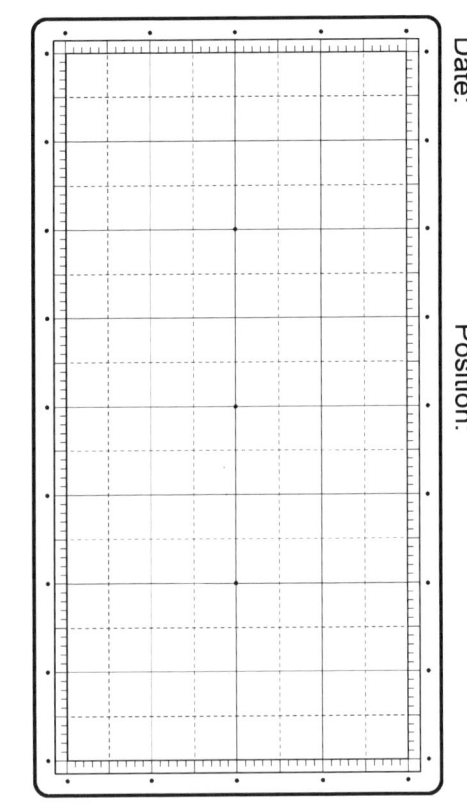

Date: Position:

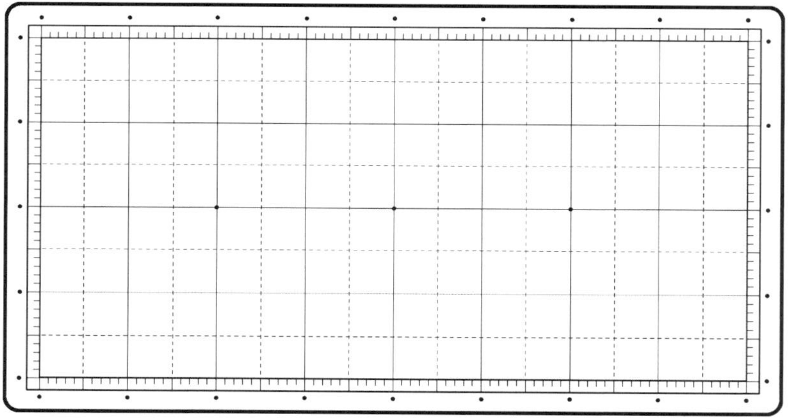

Point:

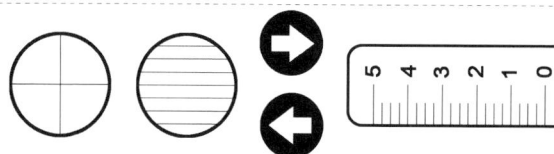

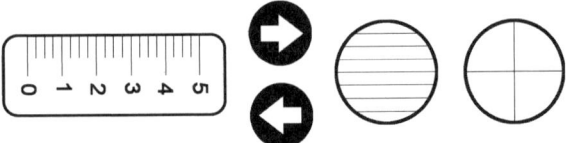

Point:

Date:

Position:

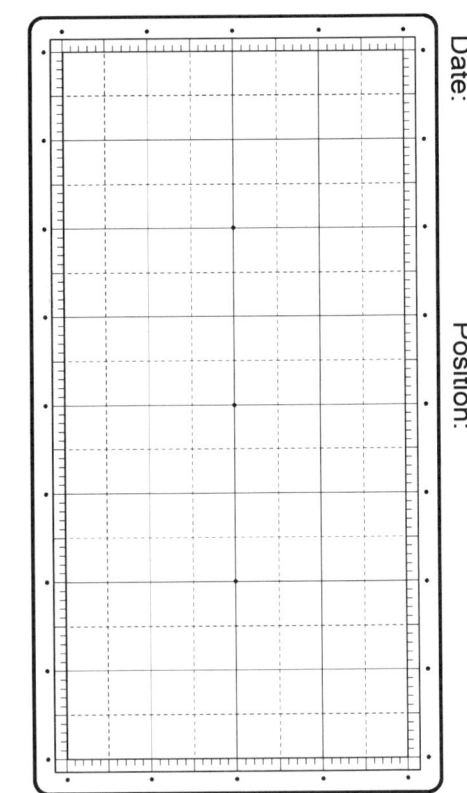

Date: Position:

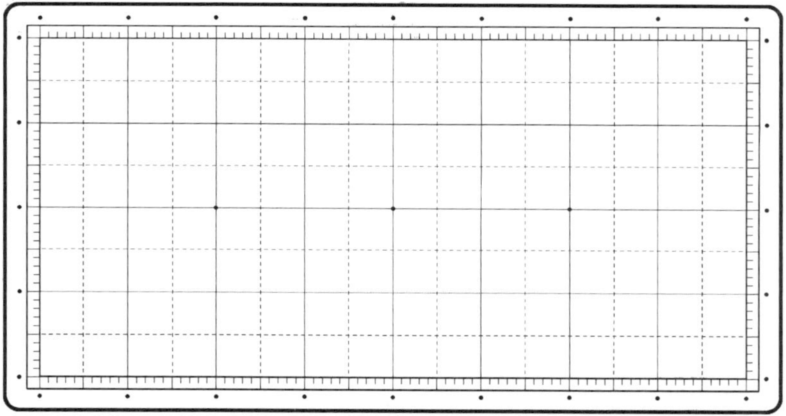

Point:

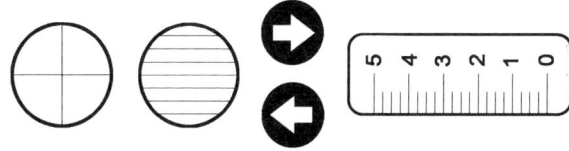

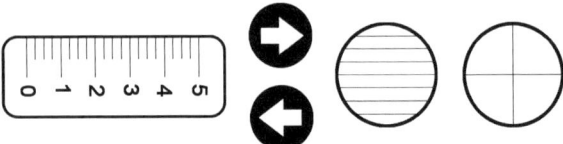
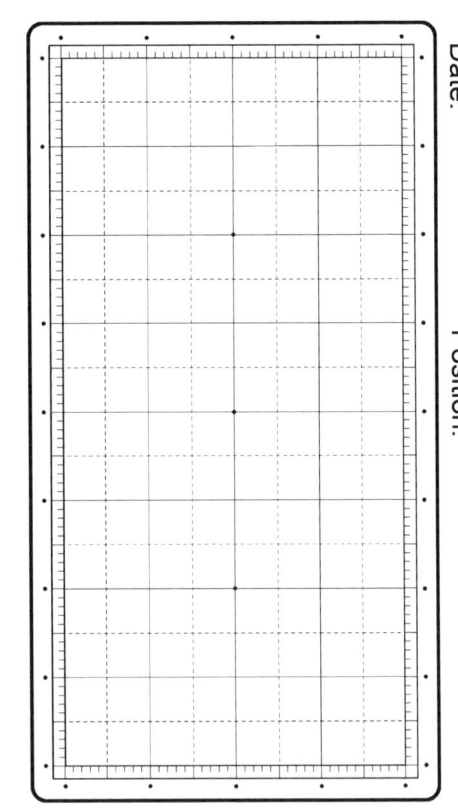

Date: Position:

Point:

Date: Position:

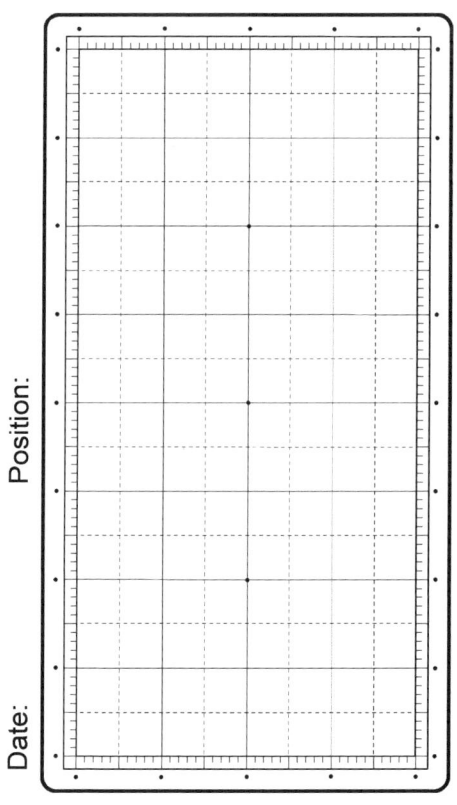

Point:

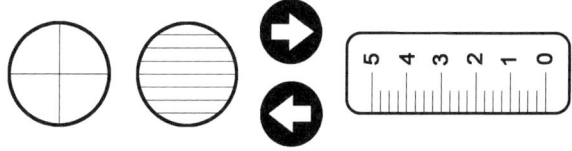

Point:

Date:

Position:

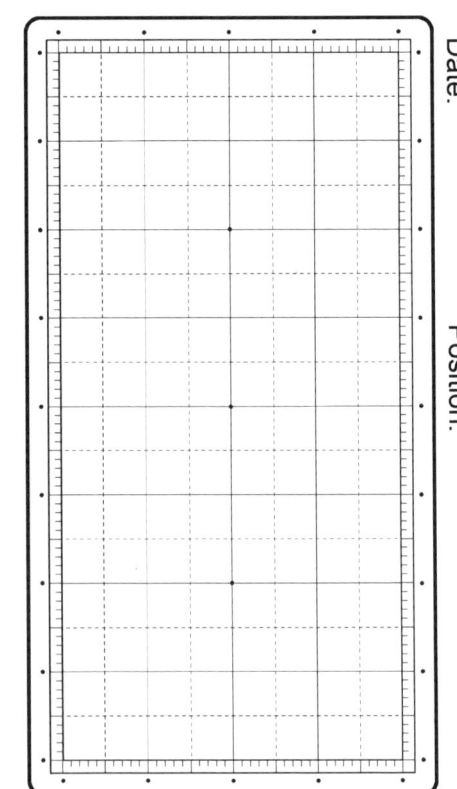

Date: Position:

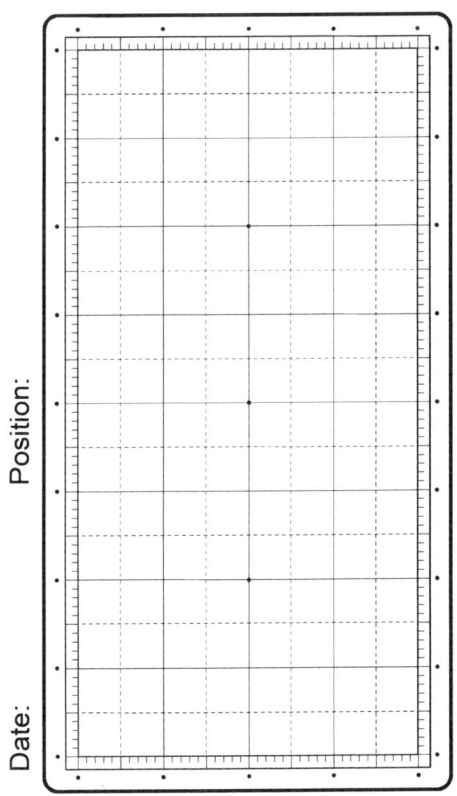

Point:

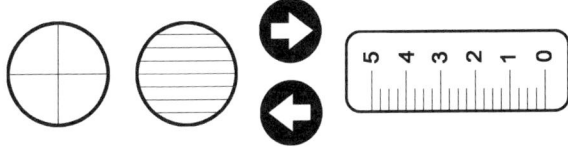

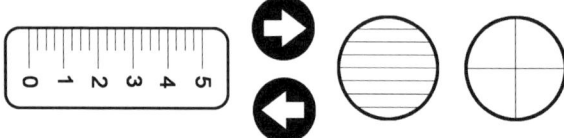

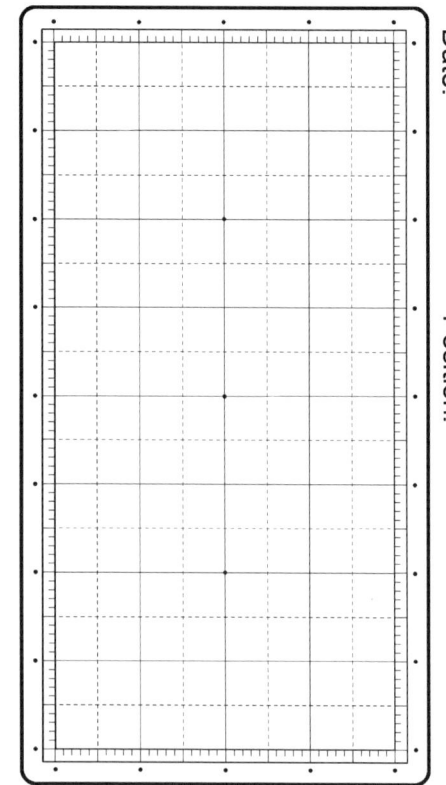

Date: Position:

Point:

Date: Position:

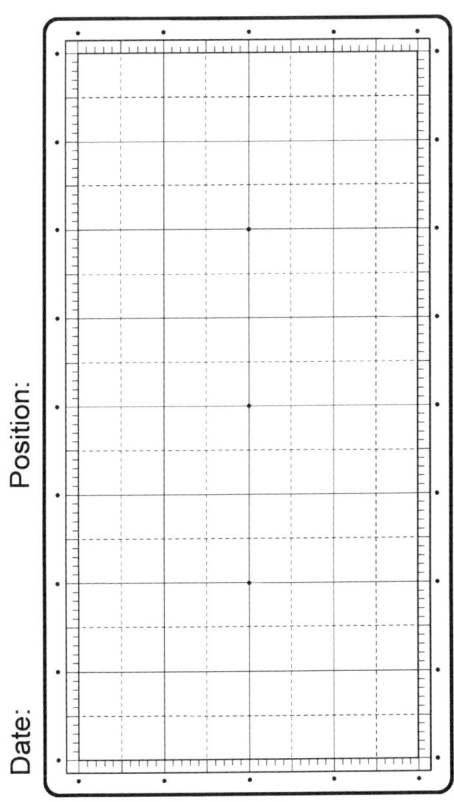

Point:

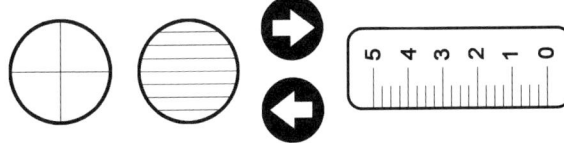

Date: Position:

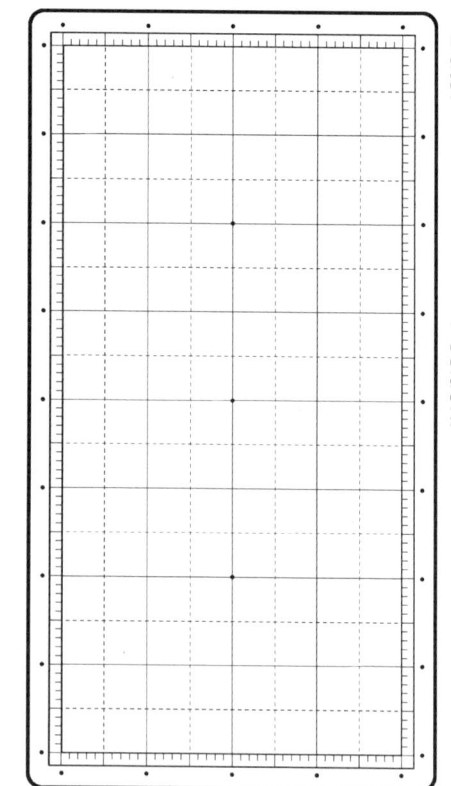

Point:

Date: Position:

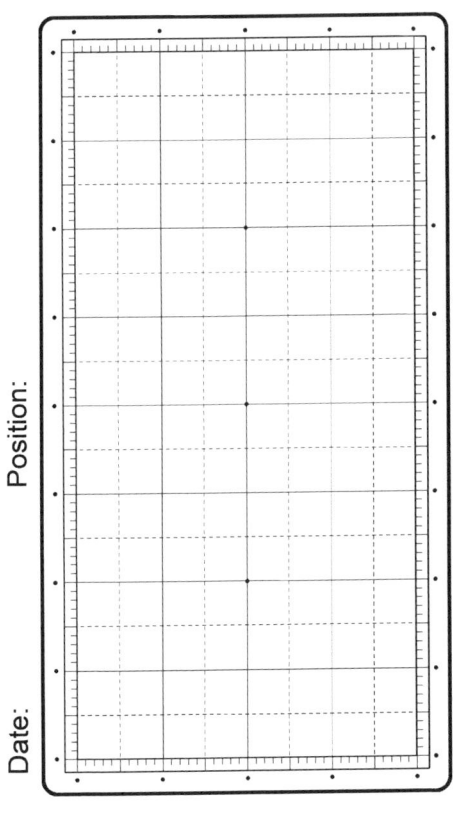

Point:

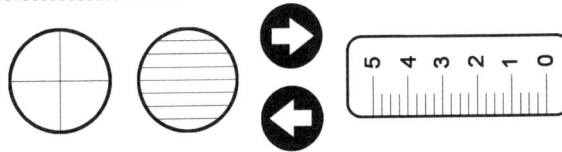

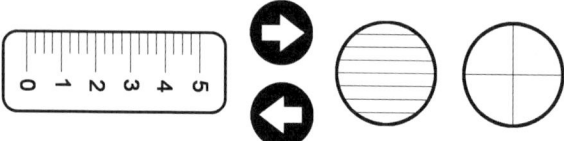
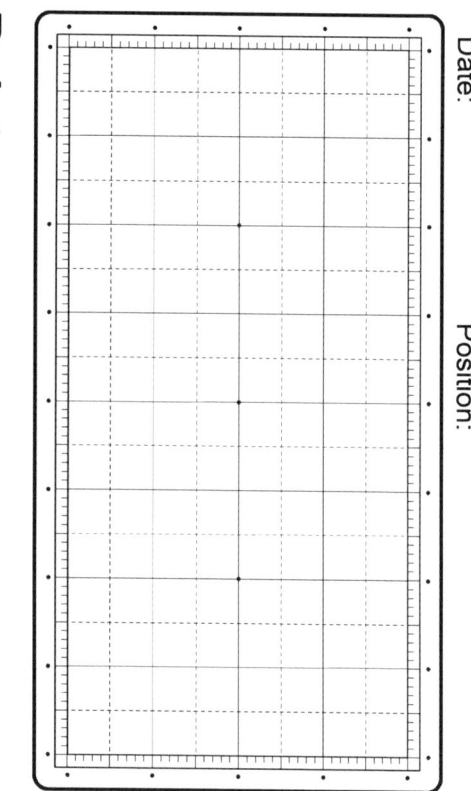

Point:

Date:

Position:

Date: Position:

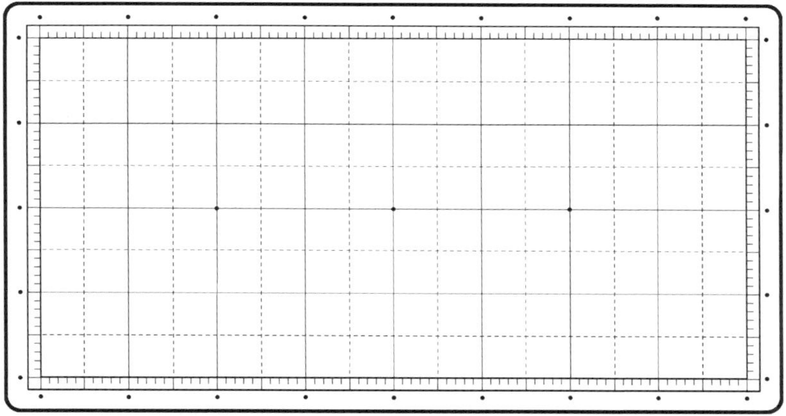

Point:

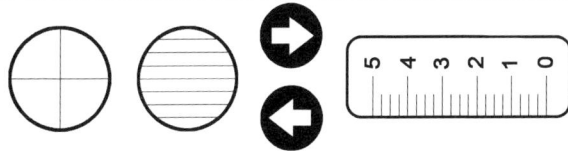

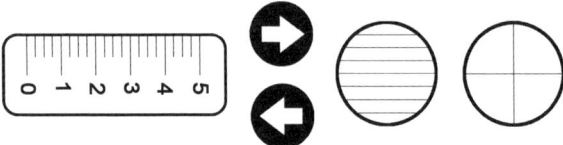

Point:

Date:

Position:

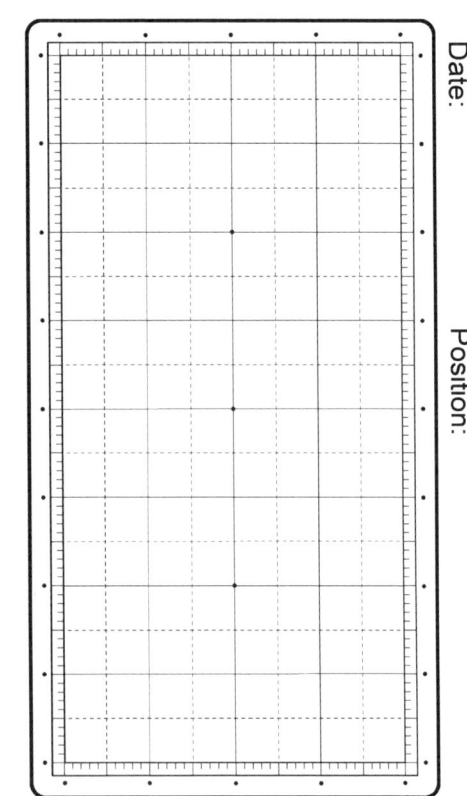

Date: Position:

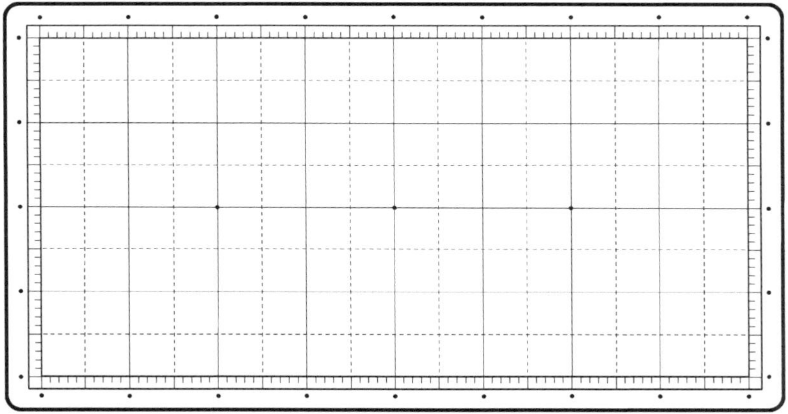

Point:

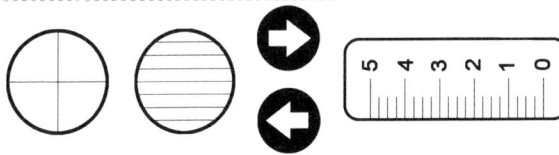

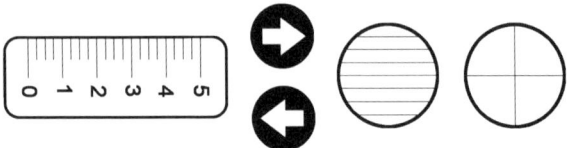

Date:

Position:

Point:

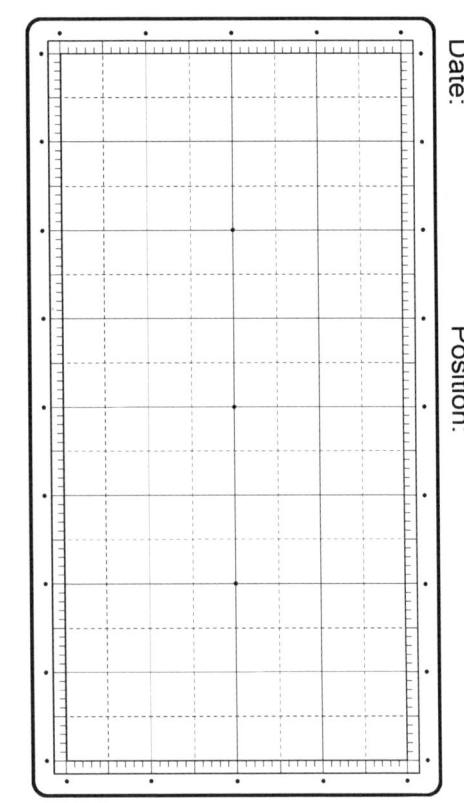

Date:

Position:

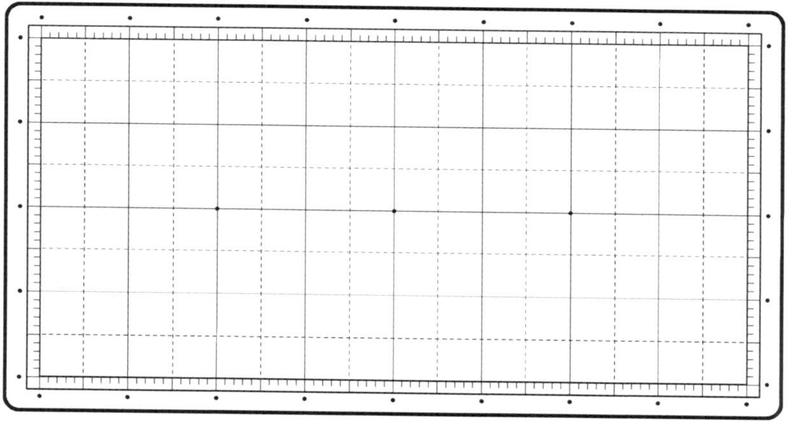

Point:

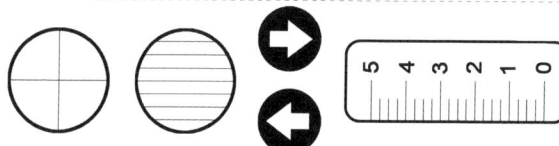

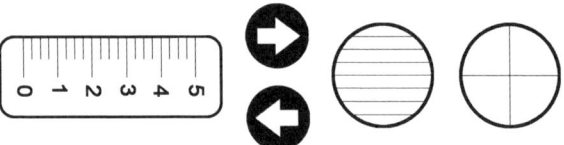

Date:

Position:

Point:

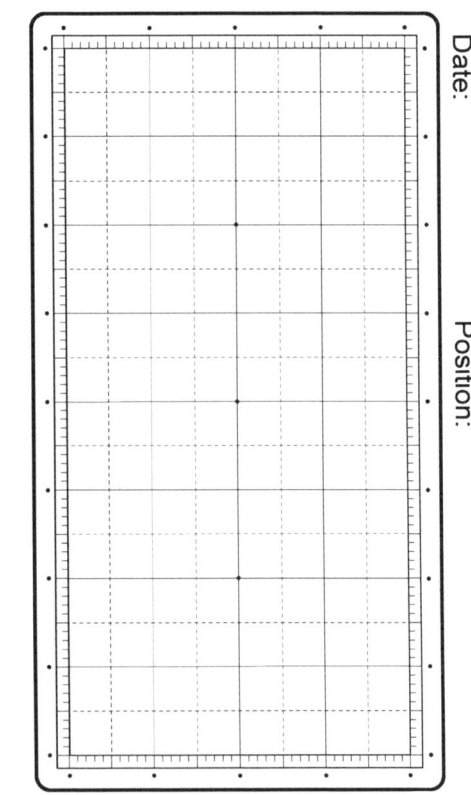

Date:

Position:

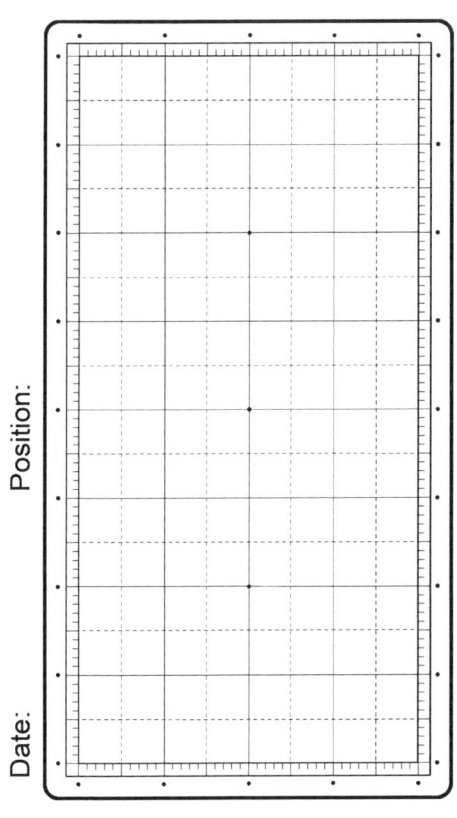

Point:

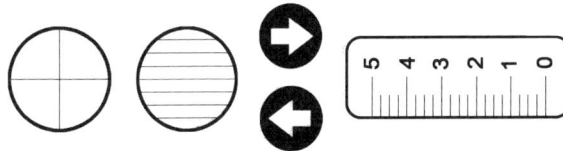

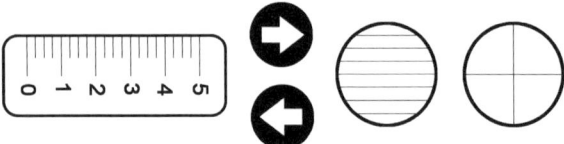

Date: Position:

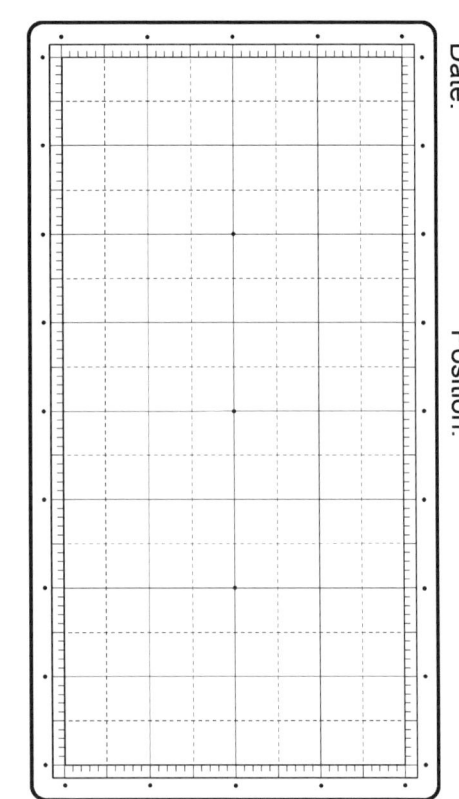

Point:

Date: Position:

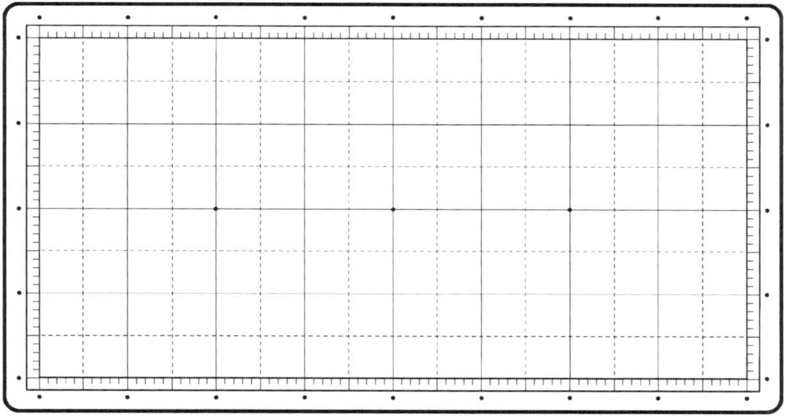

Point:

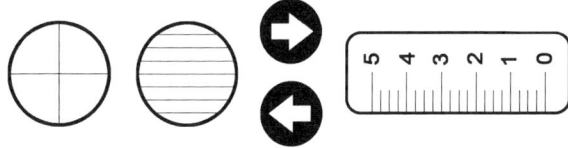

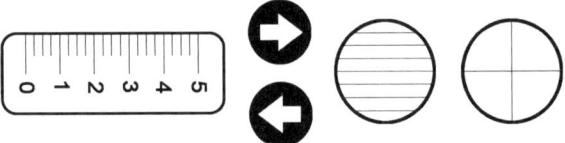

Date: Position:

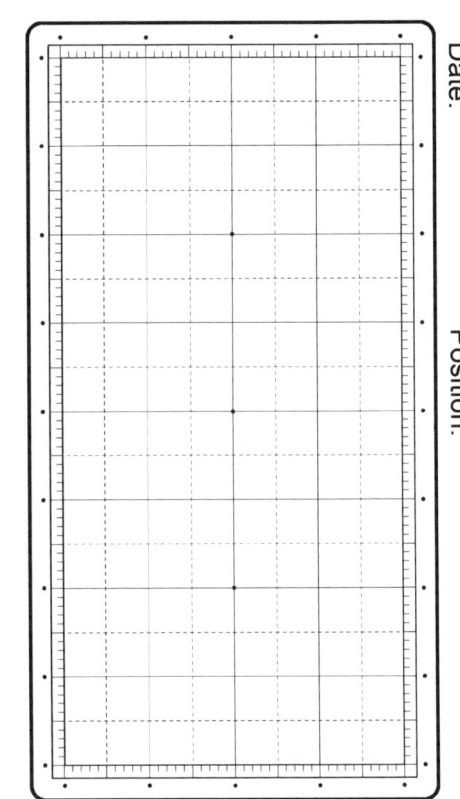

Point:

Date: Position:

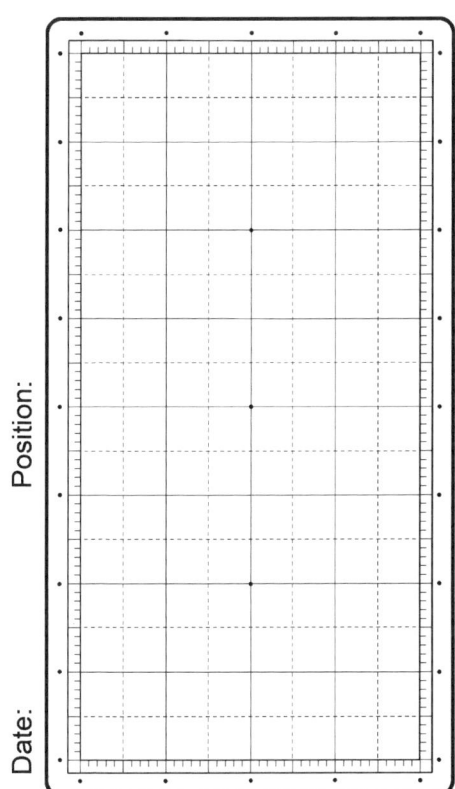

Point:

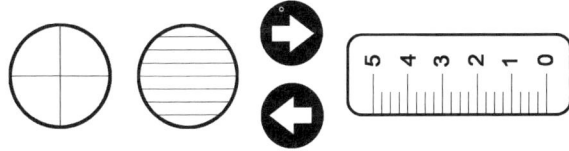

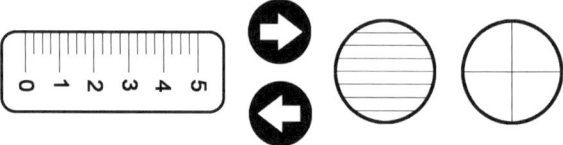

Date: Position:

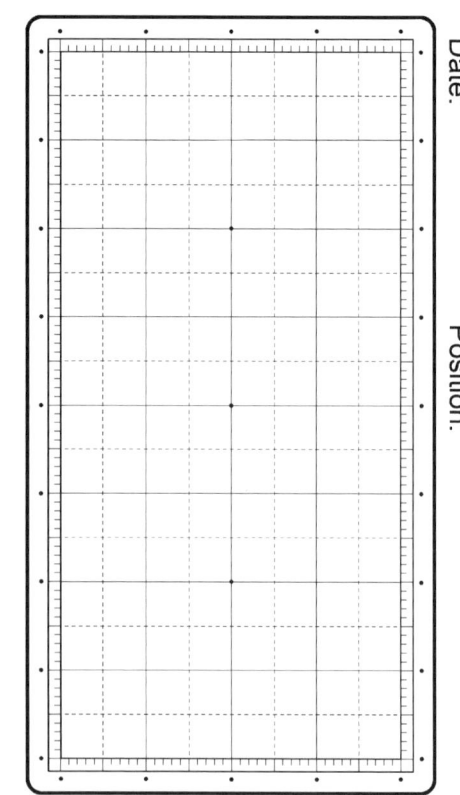

Point:

Date: Position:

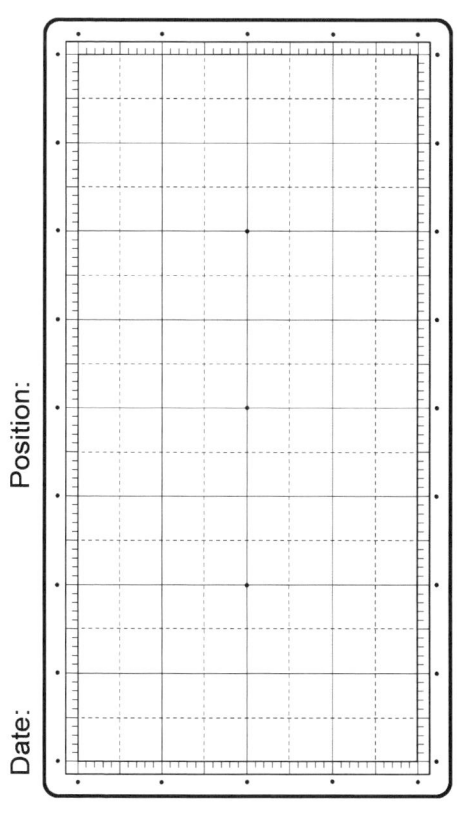

Point:

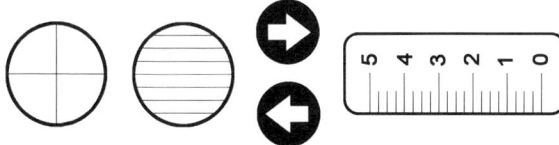

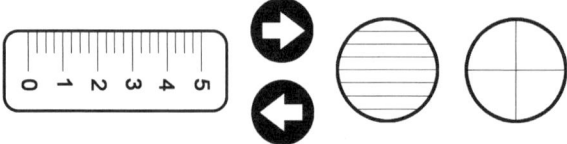

Date: Position:

Point:

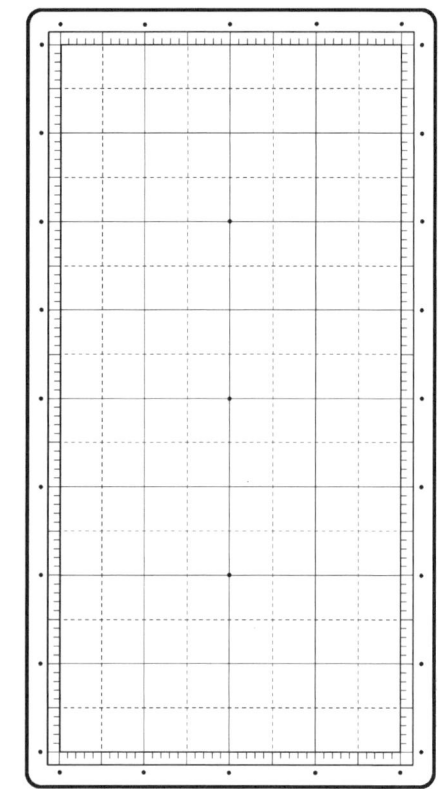

Date: Position:

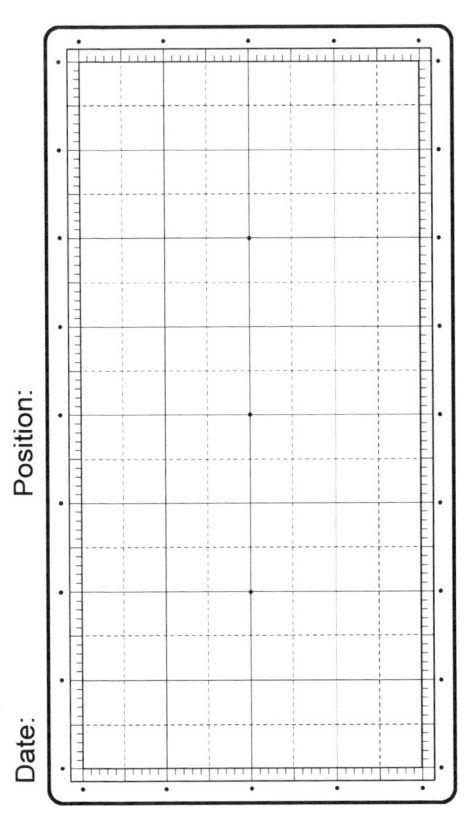

Point:

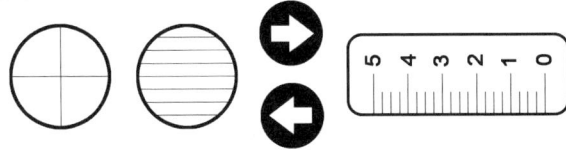

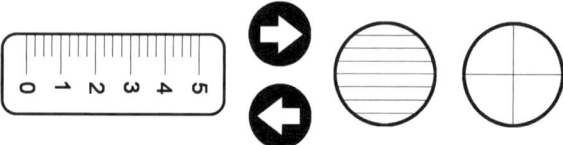

Point:

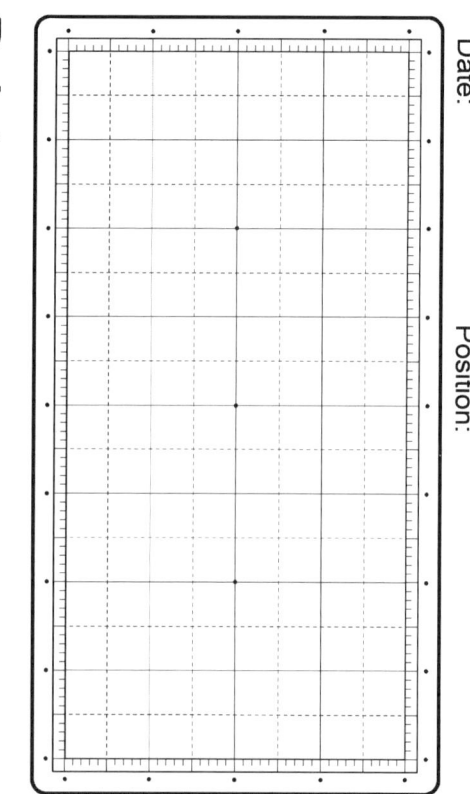

Date:

Position:

Date: Position:

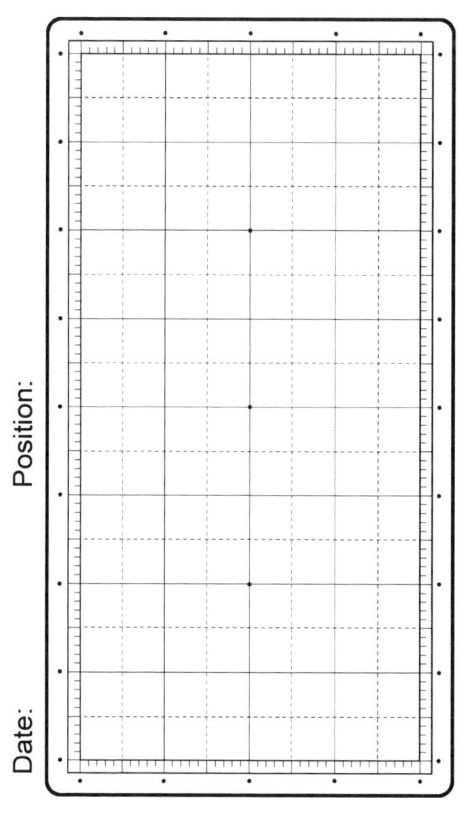

Point:

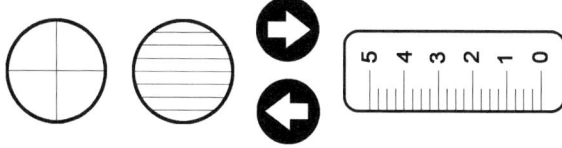

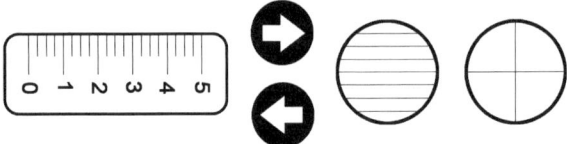

Date: Position:

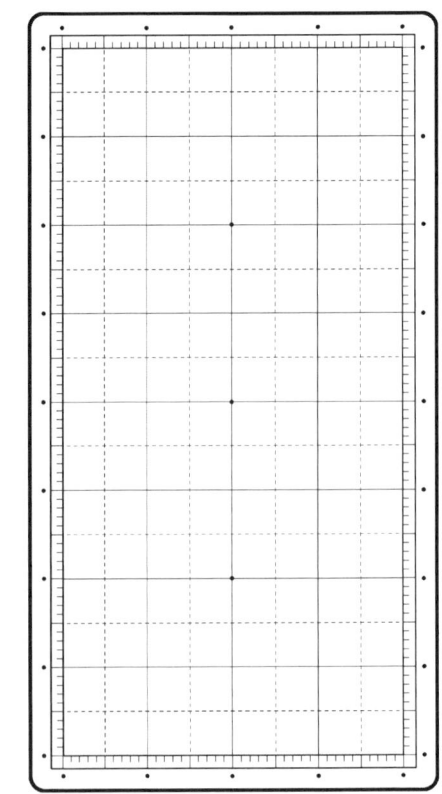

Point:

Date:

Position:

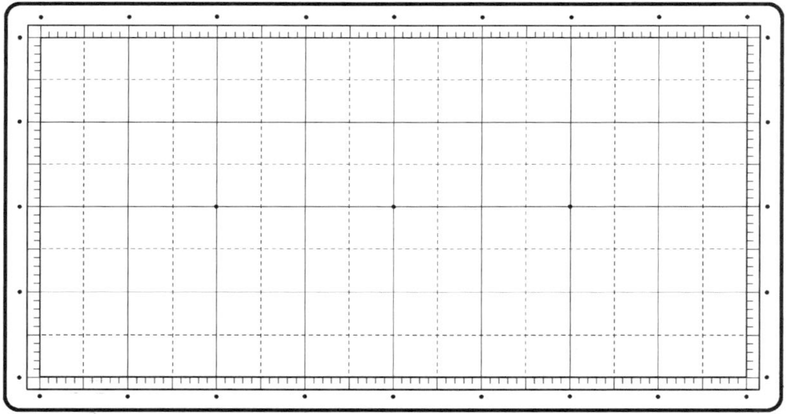

Point:

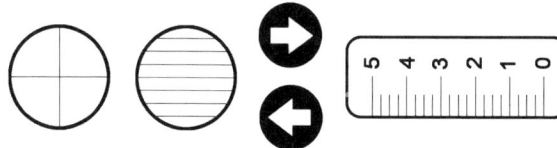

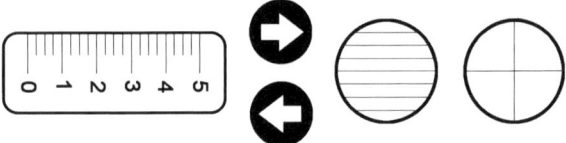

Date: Position:

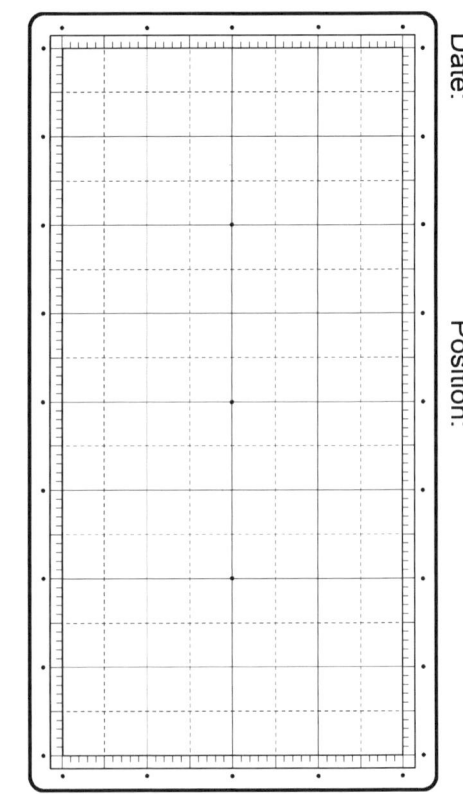

Point:

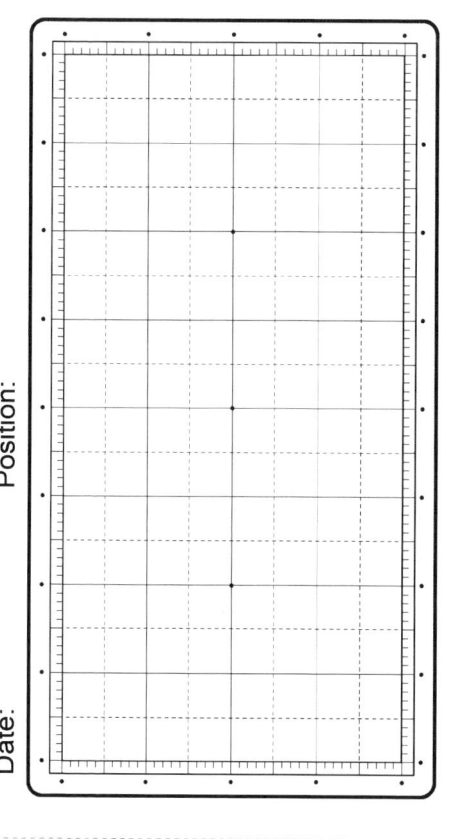

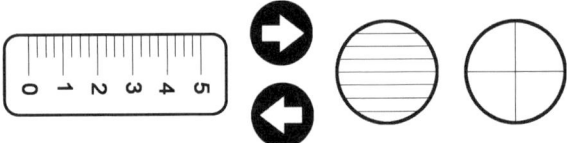

Point:

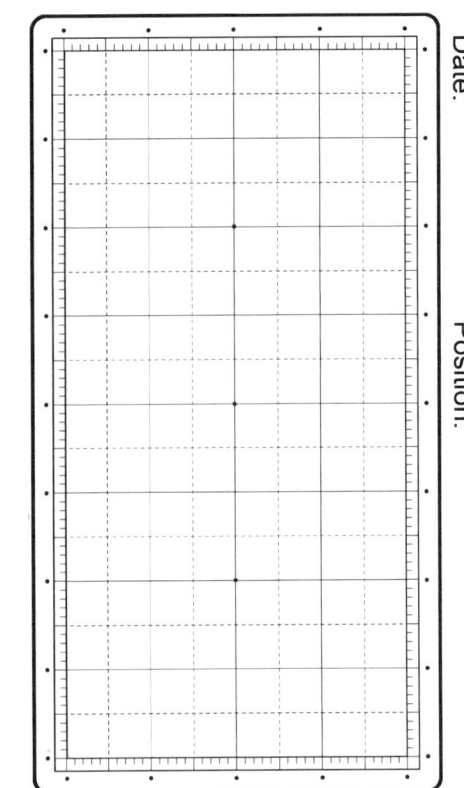

Date:

Position:

Date: Position:

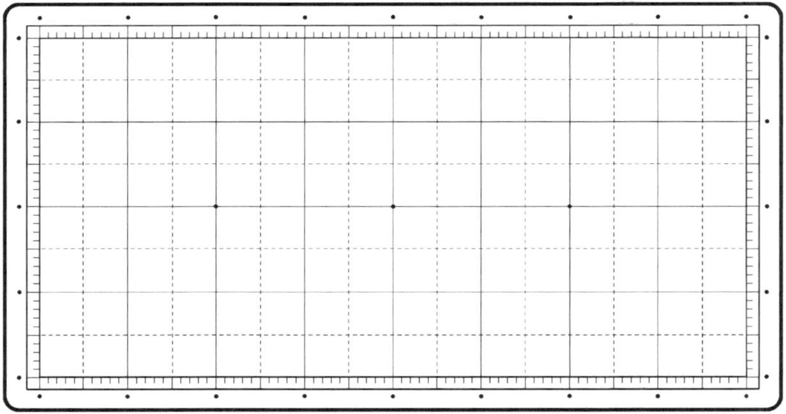

Point:

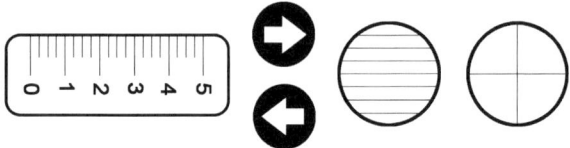

Point:

Date: Position:

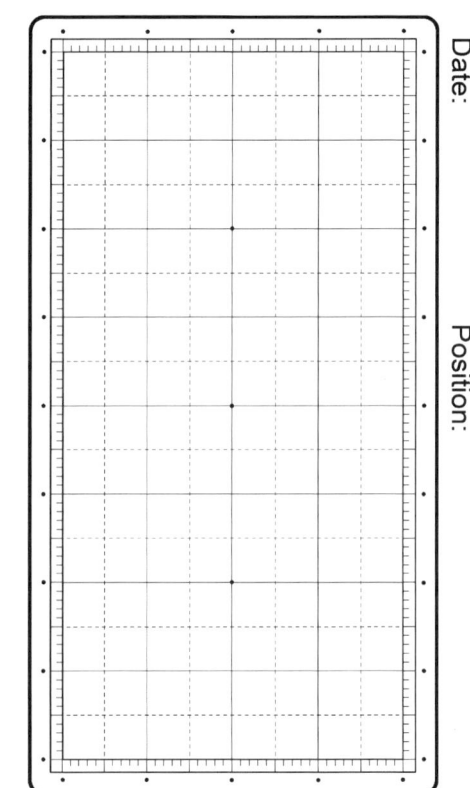

Date: Position:

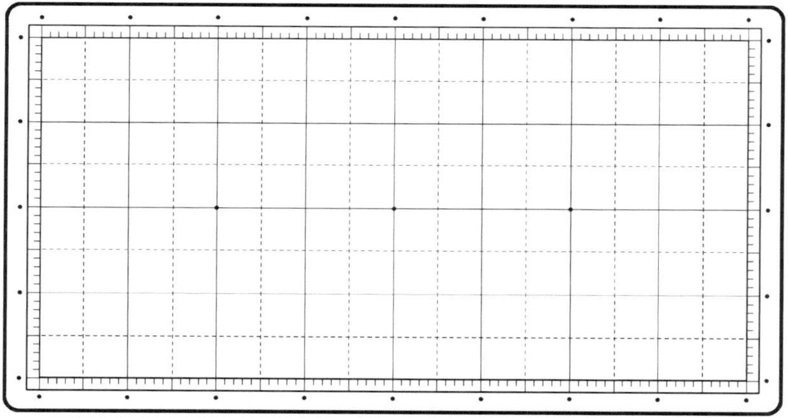

Point:

Point:

Date: Position:

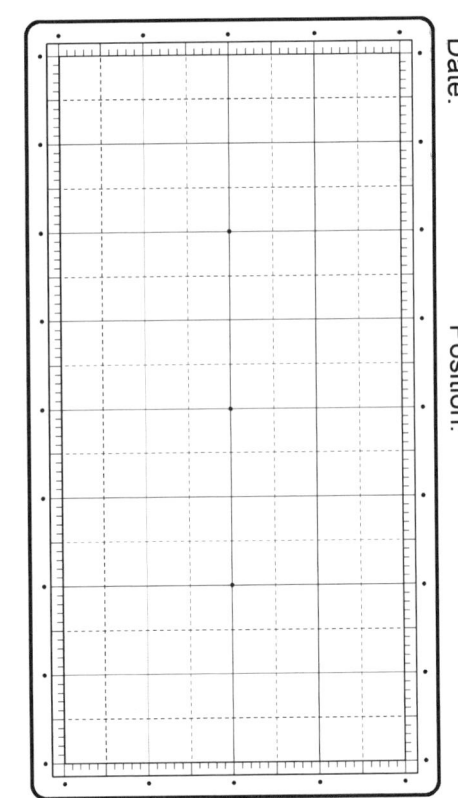

Date: Position:

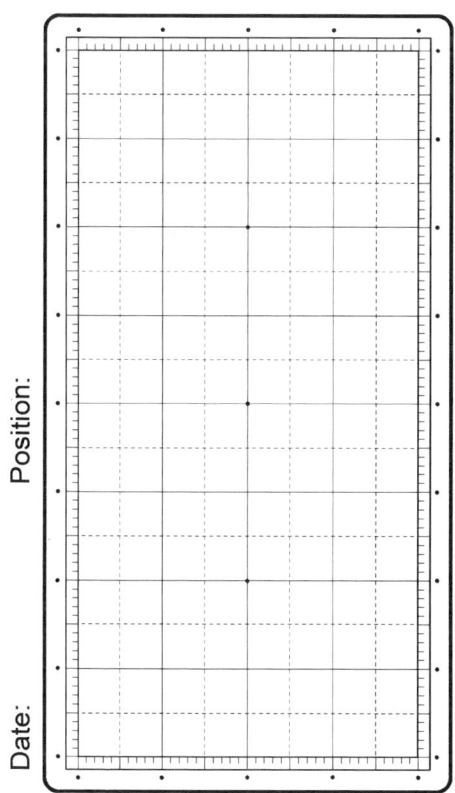

Point:

Date: Position:

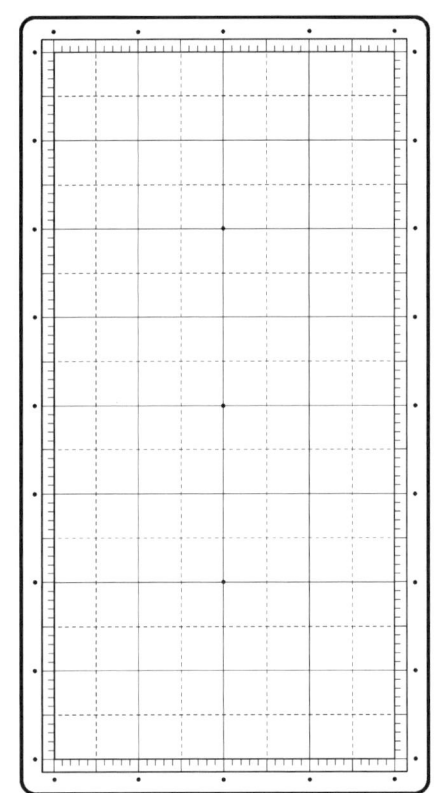

Point:

Date: Position:

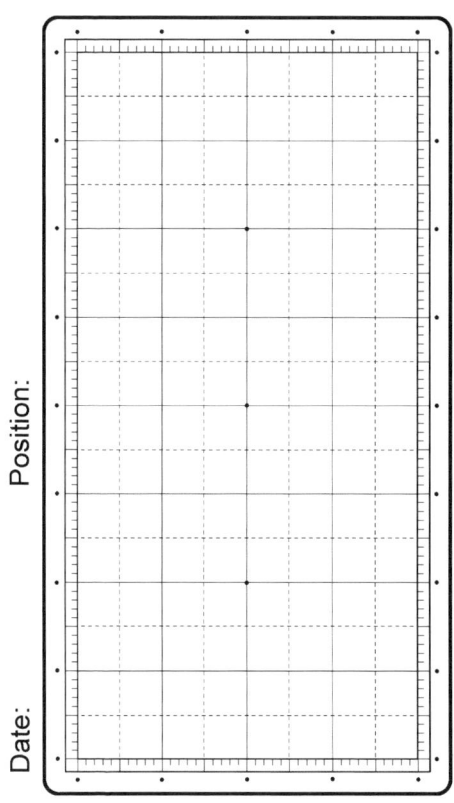

Point:

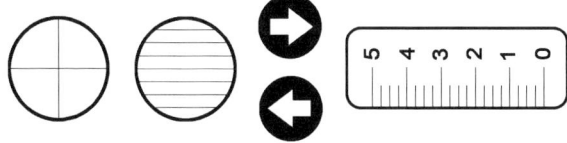

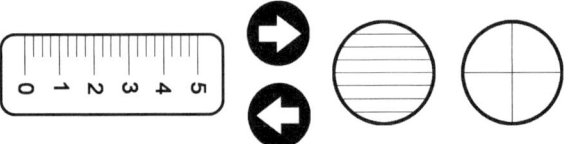

Point:

Date:

Position:

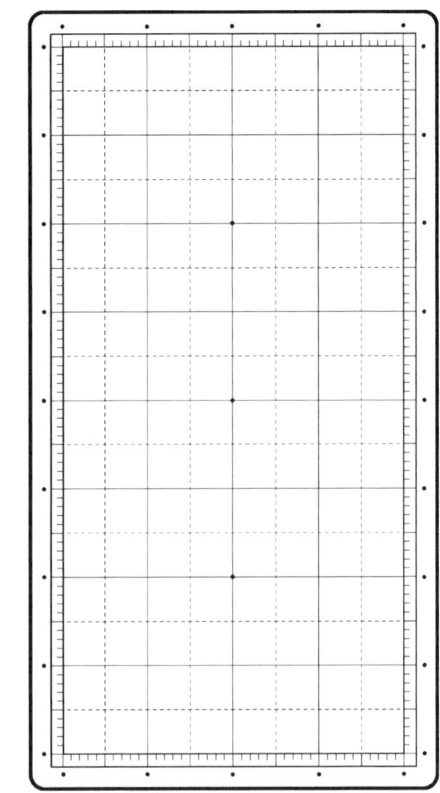

Date: Position:

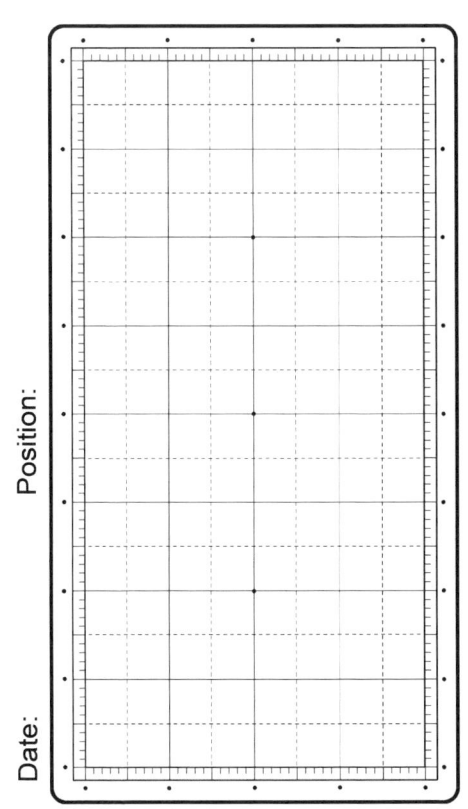

Point:

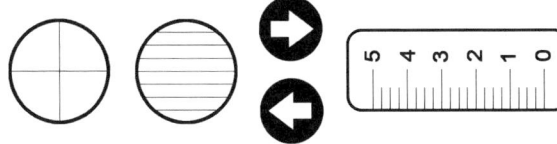

Date: Position:

Point:

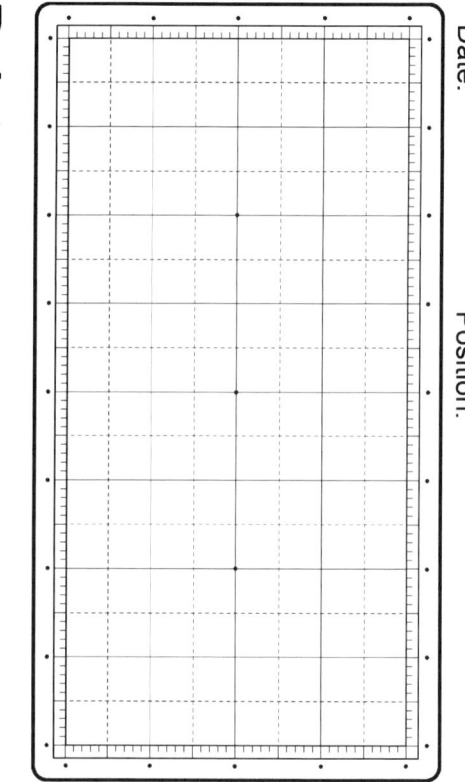

프로즌(Frozen) 되었을 때 제배치 방법
(테이블 밖으로 나갔을 때도 동일하게 적용 됨)

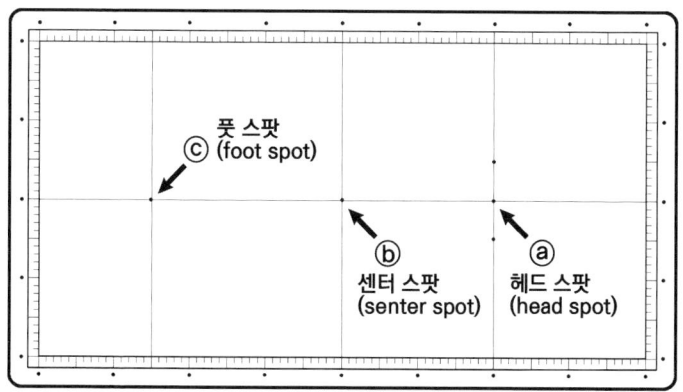

흰공(자신)의 이닝일 때

(1) 흰공(자신)과 노란공(상대방)이 프로즌 되었다면: 흰공은 ⓐ, 노란공은 ⓑ에 놓는다.

(2) 흰공과 빨간공이 프로즌 되었다면: 흰공은 ⓐ, 빨간공은 ⓒ에 놓는다.

(3) ⓐ에 다른 공이 있다면: 무조건 자신의 공을 ⓐ에 놓고, ⓐ에 있던 공을 다른 위치로 옮긴다.
   ⓐ에 있던 공이 노란공이라면 ⓑ, 빨간공이라면 ⓒ에 놓는다.
   이때 ⓑ나 ⓒ가 점유되어 있다면 둘 중 비어 있는 곳에 놓는다.

노란공(자신)의 이닝일 때

(1) 노란공(자신) 과 흰공(상대방)이 프로즌 되었다면 : 노란공은 ⓐ, 흰공은 ⓑ에 놓는다.

(2) 노란공과 빨간공이 프로즌 되었다면 : 노란공은 ⓐ, 빨간공은 ⓒ에 놓는다.

(3) ⓐ에 다른 공이 있다면: 무조건 자신의 공을 ⓐ에 놓고, ⓐ에 있던 공을 다른 위치로 옮긴다.
   ⓐ에 있던 공이 흰공이라면 ⓑ, 빨간공이라면 ⓒ에 놓는다.
   이때 ⓑ나 ⓒ가 점유되어 있다면 둘 중 비어 있는 곳에 놓는다.

3쿠션 평균 에버리지 기준표(아마추어)

30이닝 기준

G. A	Hndicap
0.3	10
0.37	11
0.40	12
0.43	13
0.47	14
0.5	15
0.53	16
0.57	17
0.60	18
0.63	19
0.67	20
0.7	21
0.73	22
0.77	23
0.8	24
0.83	25
0.87	26
0.9	27
0.93	28
0.97	29
1.0	30

35이닝 기준

G. A	Hndicap
0.29	10
0.31	11
0.34	12
0.37	13
0.40	14
0.43	15
0.46	16
0.49	17
0.51	18
0.54	19
0.57	20
0.60	21
0.63	22
0.66	23
0.69	24
0.71	25
0.74	26
0.78	27
0.80	28
0.83	29
0.86	30

3쿠션 에버리지 기록표

YEAR :

Date	Points	Inning	AVG.	HR.

3쿠션 에버리지 기록표

YEAR :

Date	Points	Inning	AVG.	HR.

3쿠션 에버리지 기록표

YEAR :

Date	Points	Inning	AVG.	HR.

3쿠션 에버리지 기록표

YEAR :

Date	Points	Inning	AVG.	HR.

3쿠션 에버리지 기록표

YEAR :

Date	Points	Inning	AVG.	HR.

3쿠션 에버리지 기록표

YEAR :

Date	Points	Inning	AVG.	HR.

3쿠션 에버리지 기록표

YEAR :

Date	Points	Inning	AVG.	HR.

3쿠션 에버리지 기록표

YEAR :

Date	Points	Inning	AVG.	HR.

3쿠션 에버리지 기록표

YEAR :

Date	Points	Inning	AVG.	HR.

3쿠션 에버리지 기록표

YEAR :

Date	Points	Inning	AVG.	HR.

3쿠션 에버리지 기록표

YEAR :

Date	Points	Inning	AVG.	HR.

Memo

Memo

Copyright© 2012~2016 by. ARA & PAULDRANG